FRANK BATTEN

Frank Batten

THE UNTOLD STORY OF THE FOUNDER
OF THE WEATHER CHANNEL

Connie Sage

University of Virginia Press | Charlottesville and London
in association with the Norfolk Historical Society

University of Virginia Press
© 2011 by the Rector and Visitors
of the University of Virginia

Printed in the United States of America
on acid-free paper

First published 2011
9 8 7 6 5 4 3 2 1

Library of Congress Cataloging-in-Publication Data
Sage, Connie, 1948–
 Frank Batten : the untold story of the founder of the
Weather Channel / Connie Sage.
    p.   cm.
 Includes bibliographical references and index.
 ISBN 978-0-8139-3155-5 (cloth : alk. paper)
 ISBN 978-0-8139-3160-9 (e-book)
 1. Batten, Frank, 1927–2009. 2. Mass media —
United States — Biography.   3. Businessmen —
United States — Biography.   4. Weather Channel
(Television station : Atlanta, Ga.) — History.
I. Title.
  P92.5.B38S35   2011
  384.55'5092 — dc22
  [B]   2010051976

To Philip

In memory of
Carl Schreiber
and
Ronald L. Speer

CONTENTS

Acknowledgments ix

Introduction 1

1 The Colonel: Samuel Slover Builds a Business 7

2 A Life of Privilege: Early Upbringing 14

3 Plebe to Commander: Batten at Culver 21

4 "Growth through Change":
   Merchant Marine and the University of Virginia 33

5 Heir Apparent 42

6 Taking Charge: The New Publisher 50

7 Putting Down Roots: Family and Community 56

8 Taking a Stand: Batten and Massive Resistance 62

9 Branching Out: The Beginning of Landmark 77

10 Legal Challenges 92

11 A Good Race: Yachting Career 100

12 A Temporary Silence 107

13 Broadening Impact: Batten as AP Chairman 114

14 "A Preposterous Concept":
    The First Year of the Weather Channel 120

15 The Weather Channel Takes Off 130

16 Landmark Continues to Grow 137

17 A Transformative Impact: Batten as Philanthropist 146

18 A Legacy Passed On 154

19 Last Years 165

Notes 173

Index 185

Photo gallery follows page 76

ACKNOWLEDGMENTS

FRANK BATTEN'S biography would not have been possible to write without the help of Norfolk Historical Society and Landmark executives Dick Barry, Walter Rugaber, Louis Ryan, and Dubby Wynne, for whose support and feedback I owe so much gratitude. I can't sing enough praises for Dick Barry's insights and skillful word editing.

I am indebted to my primary editor, Earl Swift, for his wisdom and expertise. Earl took the (many) early drafts and made them "sing," as the late *Virginian-Pilot* editor Ronald L. Speer would say.

U.Va.'s Kenny Marotta did a yeoman's job of taking the final patchwork quilt and putting it into fine shape. Thanks also to University of Virginia Press director Penny Kaiserlian, managing editor Ellen Satrom, assistant to the director Angie Hogan, and copy editor Gillian Hillis for their guidance.

I am grateful to the Batten family and to the many people throughout Landmark's businesses, TeleCable, the AP, and the Weather Channel who graciously spent hours sharing their stories. Culver Academies have earned a particularly warm place in my heart. I heap accolades on Tina Wright, Kim Kent, and Lyn Dorto Reid; their help was invaluable. And thanks also to Susan Goetz, Valary Lejman, Debbie Meads, Debbie Howell, and Carolyn Banks.

In a process that took more than a half dozen years to complete, special friends Judith Baroody, Betsy and Warren Bixler, Janice and Jack Hornbeck, Diane South, and Diane Hockenberry kept me going. Also lending their support were Rosemary Armao, Vi and George Daigler, Beth Hillson, Mary Kelly, Jean Lamkin, Beth Larmour, Lem Lewis, Dave Mayfield, Ellen Schreiber, John Schreiber, Bill Shultz, Maria Zammit, and Wendy Zomparelli.

Few have offered more wisdom—or listened to me whine more —than my sisters in our Norfolk "Reading between the Wines" book club; you're all my heroes.

A special thank you to my many wonderful friends and neighbors in Black Rock, who have been my personal rock. Also, the Journalism & Women's Symposium, the women at St. Paul's, the Inglis Fletcher Book Club, and the Girls' Breakfast Club.

The month I spent at the Ragdale Foundation artists' colony in Lake Forest, Illinois, enabled me to tackle the toughest part of the book: the chapter on massive resistance. I owe a great deal of gratitude to the entire staff.

The many friends who have written books—and made it look easy—were my inspiration, especially Earl Swift, Joe Jackson, Bob Hartman, John Rothchild, Peggy Earle, Ned Cline, Peggy Yates, Sharon and Greg Raver-Lampman, Connie Jones, Mike D'Orso, and Kay Mills.

Many of the anecdotes landed on the cutting room floor, but I could not have written this book without the help of the more than one hundred people who shared their insights. Thanks to all of you.

I interviewed Frank Batten in his home for more than 150 hours. As his health declined, it became increasingly difficult for him to talk. He did not live to see the publication of this book, but he'd be pleased, I'm sure, to know that his ethics, integrity, and values made a difference in the untold number of lives that he touched and continue to do so.

Finally, my love and thanks go to Philip Conner, my biggest cheerleader, who has infinite humor and patience. He's the captain of my ship, with whom I'm writing our own *Epilogue*.

FRANK BATTEN

Introduction

O N A H O T Saturday morning in July 1983, a half-dozen attorneys in Atlanta began a series of negotiations that would last through the night. The air-conditioning in the Trust Company of Georgia building had automatically shifted to energy-saving mode and powered down for the weekend. Tensions rose with the temperature. After pumping tens of millions of dollars into his struggling cable television network, Frank Batten was pulling the plug on the Weather Channel.

Batten knew he had been taking a big risk when he started the Weather Channel a year earlier. The brainchild of John Coleman, a weather personality on ABC's *Good Morning America,* the concept of a national weather network devoted to up-to-the-minute forecasts twenty-four hours a day, seven days a week, had gone without backers before Batten learned of it.

Growing up by the ocean, Batten believed that a weather network could save lives and protect homes and businesses. He knew the kind of terror a hurricane could wreak. When he was six years old, he was carried to safety through chest-deep water as a hurricane ripped through the mid-Atlantic, blasting sheets of seawater and sand through his family's Virginia Beach cottage and washing away two-story-high dunes. The August 1933 storm, one of the worst on record, reshaped the Maryland coastline, cutting the Ocean City inlet, which still exists today.

Batten's friends in the media were skeptical of a weather channel. "Well, Frank," said Dan Burke, president of Capital Cities/ABC, "you've got a lot of guts."[1] A nothing-but-weather network seemed like such an absurd idea that even Batten's senior managers ribbed him, crafting a "Time Channel" video spoof featuring close-ups of a large clock, its hands laboriously ticking away the seconds.

Just two years after losing his vocal cords to cancer, Batten was determined to prove his critics wrong. But as his company, Landmark Communications, Inc., poured more than $32 million into the Weather Channel, losses mounted. Advertising revenue was small; advertisers sank their cash into traditional broadcast TV, not cable programming. In the early 1980s, fewer than a quarter of American households with televisions subscribed to cable.

The leadership style of John Coleman, who had been appointed chairman, president, and chief executive officer of the network, didn't help. His bosses found him difficult and unpredictable; his employees found his behavior explosive and erratic. According to his contract, if the Weather Channel did not reach 87.5 percent of its targeted operating income in its first year, he could be fired. When Batten sought to oust Coleman from day-to-day management, Coleman secured a temporary restraining order from a Georgia Superior Court. Coleman won. Batten realized he had only one option: shut down the Weather Channel.

But Batten, who also owned a group of cable television systems, wasn't about to destroy his good reputation in the cable industry or leave Weather Channel employees in the lurch. It would cost additional millions, but he planned to give cable affiliates and employees generous notice that the network was folding. Meanwhile, Coleman made the surprise announcement that *he* wanted to buy the network. Batten agreed to give him thirty days.

In the meeting that began on July 16, details were to be worked out for the proposed sale of the network to Coleman, as well as a settlement of the court injunction. Unless a deal was worked out that weekend, Landmark was going to shut down the Weather Channel on Monday morning.

Fueled by adrenaline and caffeine, the negotiations continued for more than twenty hours. "May I borrow your pencil?" Landmark president Richard F. Barry III asked Conrad Shumadine, a Norfolk attorney who had been flown in for the negotiations.[2] Shumadine handed him a pencil. Barry snapped it in two. "That's it," he said, ending the marathon session shortly after daybreak on Sunday. A deal had finally been reached. Coleman was given an option to buy the Weather Channel. If he was unable to come up with the purchase price within thirty days, all ownership and control reverted to Landmark.

Batten, who was convinced Coleman wouldn't be able to raise the money, prepared to liquidate the network. The Weather Channel soon would be history. It would be the first time Landmark had totally failed at a venture in which Batten said it had "invested so much hope and pride as well as money."

He could not know then that the Weather Channel, dubbed "one of the most preposterous concepts on cable television," was on its way to solvency and to becoming a cultural icon. Twenty-six years later, Landmark would sell the Weather Channel for $3.5 billion. Starting the network was a risk he was certainly glad he took.

WHAT BEGAN IN 1982 as a weather service on cable television morphed into the largest private weather company in the world. The Weather Channel and its associated businesses provide weather information on every major communications platform. In the spring of 2010, the Weather Channel became the first news and information network to reach 100 million subscribers and was the second-most-widely distributed network overall. Yet few outside the communications industry have ever heard of Frank Batten, the media pioneer who started this phenomenon.

Batten's is not a rags-to-riches story. Born into a life of privilege, he inherited the controlling interest of his uncle Samuel Slover's privately held newspaper company in Norfolk, Virginia. In a career that spanned nearly a half century, Batten not only created the Weather Channel, but started TeleCable, one of the country's early cable television groups, which he later sold for $1.5 billion. Landmark Communications also owned more than one hundred daily, community, and special interest newspapers in sixteen states and two major broadcast television stations, bought and sold the Travel Channel, and co-owned the nation's largest publishers of classified magazines.

Batten simultaneously focused on winning in business and giving back to the community. As chairman of the Associated Press, in the 1980s he guided the world's largest and oldest not-for-profit news-gathering cooperative back on sound financial footing. In the midst of what he called a media marketplace "full of trash and sleaze,"[3] Batten often stood alone. In 1954, when the U.S. Supreme Court ordered public schools to integrate in *Brown v. Board of Education*, the *Virginian-Pilot*, his flagship newspaper, was the only major news-paper in Virginia to endorse court-ordered desegregation. As its publisher, Batten boldly countered Virginia's "massive resistance" to integration.

Batten forged a value-laden media enterprise rooted in decency and character. He created a company culture based on loyalty and values in an era when principles often are passé and "ethical leader" is viewed as an oxymoron. He was far from the only businessman in America with uncompromising values, of course, but with so many examples of breaches of trust in today's corporations—much of it involving media executives—he was seen by many as an anomaly.

"There's so much in the news that says to succeed you have to be a selfish bastard," said Howard Stevenson, senior associate provost for Harvard University, a professor at Harvard Business School, and a former Landmark board member. "There are many Frank Battens out there who lead quietly. With others, like Donald Trump, it's al-ways about them. With Frank it was always 'How do we make this company great?'"[4]

While some industry peers looked for short-term gains, "operat-ing like strip miners by extracting exorbitant profits,"[5] Batten cre-ated a culture of loyalty and trust by what he did and by what he didn't do. He was straightforward, principled. He set high standards for his employees. He trained, developed, and motivated his execu-tives and expected them to do the same with their workers. "His ge-nius," said former Landmark CEO John O. "Dubby" Wynne, "was in bringing out the best in people."[6] He created a collegial culture that didn't pit one person against another. He learned more by listening than by talking. He didn't micromanage, didn't constantly criticize or correct. He trusted his managers. He let them make mistakes and didn't punish them when they did. He took pride in his portfolio of businesses and their reputations.

Batten faced challenges as well. A malignant tumor claimed his vocal cords in 1979—a loss that for a national communications company owner seemed especially cruel. Not all his business ventures were successful. Although the Weather Channel survived and prospered, its European and Latin American operations failed.

Batten rejected more than one potentially lucrative business opportunity and sometimes regretted it—including a chance in the 1970s to buy the New York Yankees[7] for about $9 million; in 2010, the Major League Baseball team was valued at $1.6 billion.[8] He also "devoted a good bit of effort" to the development of a cable news network, which he dropped after being diagnosed with throat cancer.[9] He said by the time he recovered, Ted Turner "had a full head of steam on CNN."[10]

Batten's net worth kept him on the *Forbes* magazine list of the 400 Richest Americans from its inception in 1982.[11] By 2008, when his estimated net worth was $2.3 to $2.4 billion, Batten was one of the wealthiest—and least-known—men in America and one of the country's most generous philanthropists. Before his death in September 2009, Batten had quietly given away more than $400 million, nearly all of it to education.

Frank Batten is the story of a man who as a youngster was rich and rebellious. He was a low achiever with low self-esteem to match who, his uncle was warned, might become a "spendthrift playboy." Military school turned him around; business school and a series of mentors gave him self-confidence. To Batten, Slover was a daunting figure who had built his fortune on his own. After being put in charge of Slover's newspapers at the age of twenty-seven, Batten said he was determined "to prove to myself and to my uncle that I was worthy of the job he'd given me."[12]

As the media evolved in the second half of the twentieth century, Batten had a penchant for seeing developing trends well before many of his peers. He often gravitated to business opportunities that were so far down the entrepreneurial food chain that others in the industry had rejected them. By taking calculated risks, he created businesses worth billions of dollars. He was sought out for key national and local leadership roles. He gave away millions to charity and oversaw a trust fund that at its termination may be the largest gift ever received by a community foundation in the United States.

Without fanfare and limelight, he quietly built a media empire centered on integrity and ethics. Batten was successful. He was driven. Yet he struggled his entire life to prove that he was worthy of his inheritance. Throughout his life, he never felt he could live up to his uncle's expectations—and he never stopped trying.

1 The Colonel

THE STORY OF Frank Batten begins with his uncle, Samuel L. Slover. He was known as the Colonel, an honorary title given to him when he was on the staff of Virginia governor Westmoreland Davis from 1918 to 1922. Batten believed few of his own successes would have been possible without his uncle.

The Colonel was a shrewd businessman and a risk taker. When Slover arrived in Norfolk in the early 1900s, four newspapers did battle for readers, and he gambled that all four were not going to survive. He went for broke and prevailed. "There's a little bit of luck in everybody's situation," Batten said. "In most cases with the Colonel, it was his business acumen and his guts."[1] The Colonel was a pioneer whose standards Batten said he tried to live up to his entire life.

Samuel Leroy Slover was born on March 23, 1873, in Clinton, Tennessee. His father, Henry Clay Slover, was one of eleven children. Early in the Civil War, Henry and his seven brothers left their father's farm and enlisted in the Union Army. Captured in the fall of 1863, Henry was shuffled among several Confederate prison camps, including notorious Belle Isle, Virginia, and Andersonville, Georgia, where two of his brothers died. Henry was released in a prisoner exchange after thirteen months, his body wasted.[2]

He returned to eastern Tennessee to recuperate and two years later married Matilda Carden. He became constable, school commissioner, and deputy sheriff in Clinton and was elected clerk of the Anderson County Circuit Court three times.

Samuel Slover was the third of six children. While his father had been content to remain in Clinton, Sam had ideas bigger than the town and an impudence to match. As a teenager, he persuaded his father to sign a note for an option on 100,000 acres in East Tennessee. Young Sam hunted on the land but recognized its potential for coal mining. Some years later, he reportedly knocked on J. P. Morgan's door in New York to suggest that Morgan take up Slover's options. Morgan's assistant would not let Slover in to see the financier. Later, when time ran out on the option, Morgan's assistant bought the land himself.

Slover attended the University of Tennessee for a year but, eager to begin his career, left college to try his hand at real estate, then bought his hometown's small newspaper, the *Clinton Gazette*. He later jested that he was "sole owner and publisher for ninety days, the longest period for which a bank in those days would accept a note."[3] At age twenty, he was sworn in as deputy Circuit Court clerk for Anderson County, with his father as his boss.

The big city beckoned. He moved to Knoxville, taking a job as an advertising salesman at the *Journal,* and at twenty-two was business manager of the failing newspaper. Within two years, the *Journal's* circulation more than doubled. It wasn't enough: the paper owed more than $36,400 to the East Tennessee National Bank and other creditors, and Slover calculated that an additional $6,000 was needed to put the paper in the black. As the situation worsened, Slover felt responsible for the deplorable financial morass he had inherited.

Dejected, he told the newspaper's directors that the *Journal* was bankrupt. "I am frank to admit that I am absolutely helpless in the matter," he said. "My sticking to it as I have . . . has cost me, aside from worry and annoyance, loss of character and credit, and I admit to you that I feel it keenly."[4]

The paper folded. Slover left Tennessee. While he was not legally obligated to pay off the *Journal's* debt, much of which predated him, he felt morally responsible. After many years, he repaid it all.

While the *Journal* didn't survive, it was exciting to be in the newspaper trade at the turn of the century. Sensationalist stories about crime and sex were plastered across the pages of Joseph Pulitzer's *New York World* and William Randolph Hearst's *New York Journal* in a battle for circulation that became known as "yellow journalism" after Hearst raided Pulitzer's popular "Yellow Kid" cartoonist. Hysteria whipped up by the papers even was blamed for the country's involvement in the 1898 Spanish-American War.

Slover set his sights on newspapers in Norfolk. On a trip to Virginia as part of his next job selling ads in the Southeast for a New York financial journal, Slover was intrigued to find four newspapers struggling to survive. The twenty-six-year-old budding entrepreneur saw the businesses as a high-potential, high-risk opportunity, but with no money of his own to invest, he had to find a backer.

Without introduction, in 1901 Slover dropped in on Joseph Bryan, the owner of the Richmond newspapers, ninety miles northwest of Norfolk. Would Bryan stake him, he brashly asked, in buying one of the Norfolk newspapers? Bryan, astonished at the audacity, said he would not. "I really didn't think he would lend me the money," Slover later told a friend. "But I knew he wouldn't forget me."5 Slover next offered to sell advertising for the *Richmond Times*. Bryan again said no. Slover tried another tack: He told Bryan he would sell advertising on a commission-only basis, and only to new advertisers. It was an offer Bryan could not refuse.

Over the next six months, Slover's commissions were larger than the salaries of the other salesmen, the editor, and the general manager. The owners of the struggling six-month-old *Morning Herald* and *Evening Times* in Newport News, a ferry ride across the Hampton Roads harbor from Norfolk, heard about the crackerjack from Tennessee and offered Slover the job of publisher, plus a half-interest in their newspapers. The catch: he had to pull the papers out of the red in a year. Slover accepted, and the two papers successfully merged into the *Evening Times-Herald*. By 1901 he was publisher with a controlling interest.

Buoyed by his achievement, the ebullient entrepreneur next eyed the *Norfolk Public Ledger*. Slover borrowed $25,000 and with his friend Harvey Laird Wilson, a former editor of the *Times-Herald*, purchased the ailing newspaper in February 1905. Slover and Wilson had said they would pay $20,000. In his excitement, Wilson offered $25,000 and the deal was accepted. Slover suggested that he and Wilson celebrate with champagne.

"Isn't that a little rich?" Wilson asked.

"Not for a man who can give away $5,000," Slover mumbled.[6]

Slover coveted the afternoon *Norfolk Dispatch,* too, but owner James M. Thomson wasn't interested in selling. In 1906, so the story goes, Thomson was at the theater and saw Slover sitting in the balcony with Fay Martin, whom Slover was to marry in 1909. Thomson, whose health had been declining, was worried about his investments and found it hard to concentrate on the show. Slover didn't seem to have a care in the world.

"I decided then and there that if he was all that confident I'd better get out," Thomson later said.[7] Slover bought the *Dispatch* that April and merged it with the *Public Ledger* to create the *Norfolk Ledger-Dispatch.*

The following year, Slover bought the *Portsmouth Star* with his future father-in-law, Alvah H. Martin. Slover also expanded his media company with other Virginia newspapers. In 1920, he bought the Petersburg Progress Publishing Co. and the same city's Index-Appeal Publishing Co., later merging the papers to form the *Progress-Index.*

In 1923, Slover and his friend Frederick Lewis acquired a controlling interest in the *Richmond Times-Dispatch* and *Evening Dispatch.* The next year, he sold the *Portsmouth Star.* By 1926, Slover was the *Norfolk Ledger-Dispatch*'s sole owner. Two years later, he sold a majority interest in the Petersburg newspaper to Lewis for $331,275.80, to be paid over ten years. Slover kept his preferred stock valued at $165,000.[8]

During the 1920s, other newspapers attempted to break into the Norfolk market, where the evening *Ledger-Dispatch* had competed with the morning *Virginian-Pilot* since 1912. The *Norfolk Tribune* was launched in 1920 by two men from nearby Southampton County and folded forty-five days later; the *Norfolk Post* was started in 1921 by Scripps-McRae (whose name was changed to Scripps-Howard the following year) and shuttered in 1924.

On January 1, 1930, in a move the *Ledger-Dispatch* called "literally unique in the history of American journalism—if, indeed, it is not without a precise parallel in the history of American business," Slover rewarded the newspaper's top executives by giving them an opportunity to buy stock in his privately held company.[9] The Colonel gave up control of the business, but continued as chairman of the board, retaining 16 percent of its stock. The majority of the company—6,720 shares, or 67.2 percent—was sold to two families for $59.52 a share. Paul S. Huber, the newspaper's vice president and general manager, bought 3,360 shares; Frederick Lewis, Slover's partner at the *Richmond Times-Dispatch* and principal owner of the *Petersburg Progress-Index*, 2,560 shares; and his wife, Mary Lewis, 800 shares. Managing editor Henry D. Perkins purchased 150 shares, at $60 a share. Four other associates bought 25 shares each, at $60 a share. All eight paid cash for their combined 6,970 shares.[10]

The stock market had crashed only two months earlier, heralding more than a decade of worldwide economic woe, and another eight senior executives were unable to pay cash for the *Ledger-Dispatch* stock. Slover financed the sale of 1,430 shares, at $60 per share, to those *Ledger-Dispatch* executives and allowed them to pay for it on an installment plan.

Slover unveiled the plan in a December 24, 1929, front-page story headlined: "To the Friends and Readers of the Norfolk Ledger-Dispatch." The two-column announcement read, in part:

Whatever measure of success has come to the *Ledger-Dispatch* has been due in considerable degree to the fact that its personal ownership has been all but denied, certainly ignored, and that, instead, a feeling that the paper belonged to the community and was published in its interest has permeated its entire organization. That feeling, shared by all of us, has been so strong that it has impelled me to refuse many tempting offers from outside interests to purchase the property, in order that I might fulfill what I conceived to be my duty to safeguard its ownership in home people.[11]

Slover's evening *Ledger* was the stronger Norfolk paper, holding sizable leads in circulation and advertising. In the early 1930s, however, morning papers were becoming more popular and the *Pilot* started to gain circulation. The *Pilot* also had an advantage in that it boasted a Sunday edition; the *Ledger* did not.

Management at the competing *Virginian-Pilot* was in limbo. In 1898, the *Norfolk Pilot,* under owner Albert H. Grandy, had merged with Michael Glennan's *Virginian.* Ownership had been diluted over the years, leaving no majority stockholders. The *Pilot's* publisher and its general manager died within two months of each other in 1931. Slover knew the timing was right to propose a merger. The *Virginian-Pilot* and the *Ledger-Dispatch* joined forces on January 1, 1933. It was the first time since before the Civil War that the city's newspapers were controlled by one person.[12]

The merger talks also brought Slover a confidant. When a minor legal technicality threatened to become an impasse, Charles Kaufman, the *Pilot's* lawyer, called on Slover with ideas on how to resolve it. Kaufman's solution was similar to Slover's, and the two struck a deal. When Slover's attorney found out, he was so furious that he resigned as the *Ledger's* lawyer. Unfazed, once the merger was completed, the Colonel hired Kaufman as his personal attorney and the newspapers' counsel. Kaufman would later become an important advisor to Frank Batten.

Slover's commitment to his community took a more direct form with the worsening of the Depression. In 1933, one-quarter of the nation's labor force was without work. Norfolk and Southern and the Seaboard Air Line railroads, both headquartered in Norfolk, were in receivership as was the city's largest hotel, the Monticello. The local Ford assembly plant locked its doors for several months. Workers at the Norfolk Navy Yard and other government employees took a 15 percent pay cut. The city's blacks were hardest hit. In 1930, only one-third of the city's welfare recipients were black; within six years, three-quarters were. As the ranks of the unemployed swelled, the homeless set up tents in a "Hooverville" on the lawns of the city hospital.[13]

Tax collections plummeted and the city fell into the red. Norfolk Mayor P. H. Mason quit his post. Meeting that March to select his replacement on the Norfolk City Council, the five-member panel unanimously endorsed Colonel Slover without his knowledge. He had bought or bailed out newspapers in five Virginia cities. Each prospered under his guidance, but he had never held public office and only reluctantly accepted the appointment. A week later, the council asked Slover to be its president—the equivalent of mayor. Slover agreed on the condition that he receive no pay and that he be allowed to resign as soon as the city's finances were under control.[14]

He kept his word. Slover pared Norfolk's municipal budget by $500,000 and pushed through a 20 percent pay cut for municipal workers. The city's fortunes rebounded so quickly that the *News-Herald* in neighboring Suffolk suggested that Slover run for governor. He was no politician, however. His civic responsibility fulfilled, after ten months he was ready to return to his newspapers and to the responsibilities of his household, which for several years had included his wife's widowed sister, Dorothy, and her sickly six-year-old son, Frank Batten.

2 A Life of Privilege

EARLY UPBRINGING

DOROTHY MARTIN was the youngest of Fay Slover's sisters. One of eleven children born to Norfolk County Clerk Alvah Martin and his wife, Mamie, Dorothy became Fay's ward upon the death of their parents. On October 22, 1925, Dorothy —a tall, plain, shy twenty-two-year-old who had attended Hollins College in Roanoke, Virginia—married Frank Batten, who would give his name to his son. A handsome and gregarious twenty-eight-year-old, he had attended Washington and Lee College in Lexington, Virginia, for one year, served in the Army in World War I, and worked in Norfolk as an auditor for Virginia National Bank.

The couple's only child, the younger Frank Batten, was born on February 11, 1927, during the worst blizzard Norfolk had witnessed in decades. A year later, on March 31, the elder Batten died of lobar pneumonia. He was thirty-one. His widow and son moved in with the Slovers. The childless couple welcomed the toddler despite his profound effect on their very adult household; Fay was not quite forty-three years old when Frank was born, and the Colonel, fifty-four. Frank's bouts of asthma landed him in hospital oxygen tents, the standard treatment for the respiratory disorder in the 1930s. At the Slovers' he would be cared for by his mother, aunt, and uncle—not to mention his nanny, Lugie, a small woman in her twenties—along with cooks and maids and Mattu Collette, his uncle's driver and manservant. Frank Batten had entered into a life of privilege, wealth, and power.

The Slovers were one of the most affluent families in Norfolk. They had the wherewithal to spoil their nephew, even during the darkest days of the Depression. Frank had model boats and battleships, baseball gloves, roller skates, and bicycles, which became his favorite toys after his stuffed animal, "Pink Monkey," wore into a heap of wires and fuzz. He had his own radio in his bedroom, the walls of which were decorated with sports pennants. Fay Slover kept a special gift closet packed with marionettes, dolls, and other birthday and Christmas presents she bought at New York's FAO Schwarz toy store for her nephew and his cousins.

Those five girls, dressed in holiday velvet dresses, joined the annual Christmas celebration, highlighted by an electric train chugging on its tracks in the Slovers' attic playroom, by a towering, floorto-ceiling Christmas tree, its branches trimmed with candles, bells, and ornate imported glass ornaments, and by the aroma of steaming hot homemade rolls and turkey, goose, and wild duck from the Colonel's private game reserve.[1]

Several of Batten's summers in the 1930s were spent at Greenbrier Camp for Boys in West Virginia's Allegheny Mountains (from which he sent a brief, unusually formal request of his mother just before one Fourth of July: "Dear Mrs. Batten: Please send me fireworks. Sincerely yours, Frank Batten Jr.").[2] After six weeks at camp, Frank joined his family at the Slovers' oceanfront cottage in Virginia Beach. The family typically didn't return to Norfolk until October, well after the new school year was underway.

One autumn morning when he was about ten years old, Fay Slover drove her nephew to school in the family's sleek, dark green Packard. The luxury car sold for $3,500 during the Depression, at a time when the average worker's annual salary—assuming one could find work—was $1,368. Frank was self-conscious about his family's wealth and did not want his pals to see him step out of a vehicle fit for a prince. He asked his aunt to drop him off a couple of blocks away from Robert E. Lee Elementary School and walked the rest of the way.

Frank called the Colonel "Umpity," a holdover from the days when, as a toddler, he couldn't pronounce "Uncle." Slover cut an imposing figure. Ramrod straight, he looked taller than his five feet ten inches. A square face and ruddy complexion framed piercing eyes. He dressed formally both at work and at home, wearing conservative blue or gray suits over his broad chest and thirty-nine-inch waist. About town, the balding Slover sported a straw boater or a stylish wool fedora trimmed with a band of grosgrain ribbon. He walked with a gentleman's cane and was rarely without a cache of Cuban cigars.

Smoking one of those thick, hand-rolled cigars, purchased on a trip to Havana, and sipping a glass of Hudson Bay scotch, Slover enjoyed telling Frank stories of his career. One tale was set at the turn of the twentieth century, when the *Times-Herald*, Slover's Newport News newspaper, was in the midst of a circulation war. To lure readers, his editors plastered stories across the front pages announcing doom and gloom or thrilling to the latest scandal. One series blasted a municipal contractor for allegedly defrauding the government.

After days of banner headlines, Slover received a telephone call at his office from a friend with alarming news. The contractor, enraged by the stories, had a gun and was on his way to the newspaper. The Colonel hung up the phone, pulled his own pistol out of a desk drawer, and calmly waited for the showdown. High noon came and went, but the contractor never showed.

Some of the Colonel's tales were cautionary. He told Frank about sponsoring a slogan contest for the *Ledger-Dispatch;* the winning motto announced with great fanfare: "Truth, Justice, and Public Service." Slover soon learned that this was the slogan for a Hearst newspaper.

Another *Ledger-Dispatch* promotion saw a fast-talking peddler come through town promising to stuff money of varying denominations into colorful balloons and set them free on a given day. With plenty of advance publicity, crowds of subscribers and would-be subscribers gathered at the newspaper to watch the balloons float skyward. As the balloons slowly drifted back to the ground, men, women, and children chased after the floating piggy banks and with great jubilation popped the balloons. They were empty. By then, the balloon booster had disappeared with $500 of the Colonel's money.

Frank experienced for himself a promotion of his uncle's that was more successful. For the first half of the twentieth century, newspapers were the town criers, delivering news, weather, and information. Readers rushed to the sports pages to check the latest scores. A baseball fanatic, Colonel Slover wanted to share World Series scores hours before his papers landed on subscribers' front porches. He hung an electronic scoreboard on the *Ledger-Dispatch* building so fans could follow the series action as it happened. The elaborate, brightly illuminated sign flashed when a player was at bat, showed how many strikes and balls were pitched, and indicated who was on each base. It was so popular that traffic was blocked from downtown Norfolk's Plume Street. It wasn't mere altruism; he saw it, too, as a way to boost circulation and community good will, presaging marketing campaigns that would later create brand equity, build customer relationships, and target audiences in the news and other industries. One of Frank's earliest memories was "watching" the October 1934 World Series game in which Dizzy Dean pitched the St. Louis Cardinals to an 8-3 victory over the Detroit Tigers. It was Frank's introduction to "electronic media."

In the evenings, Frank often joined his uncle to listen to the family's RCA radio in the first-floor library. The Colonel always sat in his favorite plush upholstered chair in a corner beside a large fireplace. The family listened not only to *Your Hit Parade* and the *Chase and Sanborn Hour* with Edgar Bergen and Charlie McCarthy, but to the news commentaries of H. V. Kaltenborn, who would later visit the Slovers, and to the boxing matches of Joe Louis. Frank accompanied his uncle to Yankee Stadium to watch Louis defeat Tony "Two Ton" Galento in 1939. The trip inspired a home-made match in the Slovers' large attic playroom, inside a ring strung with rope. Tickets were sold to parents and neighbors at 25 cents apiece. A parent served as a referee, calling rounds with a cowbell, remembered E. Bradford "Brad" Tazewell Jr., who remained one of Batten's closest friends. The ten or fifteen dollars the boys raised went to charity.

A mediocre athlete himself, Frank loved going to any sporting event with his uncle, who was happy to take him. Duke University's football team was invited to play Oregon State in the 1942 Rose Bowl. After the Japanese bombed Pearl Harbor on December 7, 1941, the

New Year's Day game was moved across country from Pasadena, California, to Durham, North Carolina. Frank and his uncle joined 55,000 spectators who sat on bleachers borrowed from the University of North Carolina and North Carolina State University. Duke, undefeated and heavily favored, lost to Oregon State on a cold, rainy day.

The Colonel had tickets to World Series games if the Yankees were playing, and Batten became a lifelong Yankees fan. Many star players, including Yogi Berra, Phil Rizzuto, and Whitey Ford, got their start with the Norfolk Tars, which became a farm team of the Yankees in 1934.

Frank hunted with his uncle, too, starting out with a lightweight .410-gauge shotgun, then graduating to a 12-gauge. The Colonel was one of several owners of the Ragged Island Gunning Club, reputed by many as among the finest duck shooting properties on the East Coast. It was one of several clubs in the Back Bay section of what today is Virginia Beach, most owned by wealthy gentlemen hunters from New York and Philadelphia. The clubs eventually would be taken over by the federal government; today they are part of the 8,000-acre Back Bay National Wildlife Refuge.

In 1939, the Colonel paid $9,000 to scoop up another hunt club, consisting of 1,000 acres, one and a half miles of Atlantic Ocean beachfront, and several miles of marsh. In recognition of his zeal for the sport, the False Cape Gunning Club was deeded to the boy when he was ten years old, although Frank would not learn about this until long after. Like the Ragged Island club, False Cape eventually was taken by the government: Virginia turned the land into a state park. Its maritime forests and old dunes today are one of the few remaining undeveloped areas along the East Coast with a large migratory bird population.

Fay Slover served as young Frank's disciplinarian. Short, with wavy hair framing a heart-shaped face and sparkling eyes behind her wireless spectacles, Fay was outgoing, smart, and personable. If she had lived in a different time, her nephew said, she would have been the CEO of a company. She dominated Frank's mother, who obsessed about her weight and subsisted on fresh vegetables and rye crisp crackers. Dorothy Martin Batten was probably anorexic, her son would come to believe. A childhood friend remembered Dorothy as stiff and distant. Frank remembered her as unfailingly kind, thoughtful, and generous, although too tolerant of his many youthful indiscretions. Dorothy was happy to let her sister handle the discipline. Even so, Frank was rarely punished, even after he was expelled from three schools.

Until his early teens, Frank lacked focus and discipline, disliked school, and was on a path that promised heartache. He would later describe himself as pudgy, a poor reader, and a mediocre athlete who went along with whatever his older pals did. A friend of the family warned the Colonel that his nephew might end up being a "spend-thrift playboy."

When Frank and his friends weren't playing kick-the-can or sand-lot baseball, they were getting into trouble. Some of the pranks were fairly harmless. Others were serious. They shot out street lights with slingshots and BB guns, siphoned gas from cars, and greased trolley tracks, derailing cars.

Norfolk lawyer Thomas G. Johnson Jr. said he grew up hearing tales of the boys' misdeeds, including the time they set a field on fire near the Hague Club, a private dance hall near the Slover house. The blaze got out of control, the club caught on fire, and everyone in it was forced to evacuate. Frank and his buddies also wrecked the interior of a vacant palatial brick house in the neighborhood that had been repossessed after the 1929 stock market crash. For years the Bruce house, as it was known, had been boarded up. Even though it was across the street from the Slovers', it was an irresistible target for juvenile delinquents, and they were never caught.

"We spent about four years destroying it," Batten said. "We broke every chandelier, every piece of glass they had"—using, among other things, crowbars. A wall safe on the second floor was particularly intriguing to the boys, who in hopes of reaching the valuables inside tried unsuccessfully to purchase nitroglycerin from their local pharmacy. The boys also kept a tin of tobacco stuffed in holes of the lattice work covering the brick walls at the servants' entrance, and once were nearly caught as they smoked on the roof of the mansion's small porte-cochere when a police car, on the lookout for vandals, drove right under them.

Batten later attributed his waywardness to immaturity. He was the youngest in his gang, and his insecurity made him a follower.

Frank not only was part of a rowdy gang of kids, he was a troublemaker in school. A self-described lazy student, he attended public primary schools in Norfolk, transferring to private Norfolk Academy for the sixth and seventh grades. Neighborhood kids taunted Academy students, calling the school the "day nursery" and the "sissy school." Batten didn't like it either. One day, a teacher notorious for whipping the kids with a switch stepped out of the room. When he returned, he found Frank sitting on the classroom's first floor window ledge and came after him with the stick. Batten jumped out the window. He was suspended for a week.

He preferred public school because most of his friends were there. In the eighth grade at Blair Junior High School, Batten and his pals skipped school several times to go bowling. Eventually they were caught, and his mother had to go with him to the principal's office. She was not amused, especially after he finally confessed that he had been a truant on multiple occasions to bowl duckpins. He was booted from that school, too, though this time for only one day.

Frank was about to enter the ninth grade. With his less-than-stellar academic record, his mother, aunt, and uncle considered sending him to Episcopal or Woodberry Forest, both Virginia boarding schools. Maybe shipping him off to a private high school, away from home, would straighten him out.

Frank had another idea.

3 Plebe to Commander

I N 1939, TWELVE-YEAR-OLD Frank was captivated by *The Spirit of Culver,* a film starring Jackie Cooper and Andy Devine. It told the tale of an orphan who won a scholarship to Culver Military Academy in Culver, Indiana, and of a cocky student whose arrogance and unwillingness to comply with the academy's strict rules landed him in hot water.

Culver, founded in 1894, was the country's largest military preparatory school. Half of its more than 3,500 graduates had served in World War I. Eighty-six alumni had died in the War to End All Wars. The movie inspired Batten, who imagined himself in a snappy full-dress Culver uniform: white trousers, gray coat, and leather shako —a tall military cap with a white pompon.

Boys were most attracted to Culver because of its uniform, noted *Life* magazine in a June 1939 feature story about the school. The attire was a nuisance at school but had a "wonderful effect on girls."[1] The Culver regalia also had an effect on boys like Frank Batten, who dreamt of being a real warrior instead of playing games with tiny wooden soldiers.

On Christmas Day 1939, H. P. McNeal Jr., the owner of Norfolk's Empire Machine Tool Co., paid a courtesy call at Colonel Slover's home. With him was his son, Sonny McNeal, sharply dressed in the tailored, charcoal gray wool uniform of a Culver cadet. A dark tie was tucked in his army-style jacket and he wore a soft wool garrison cap. The cadet was well-mannered, polished, and stood erect as a warrior.

For the undisciplined young Batten, this squared-away teenager looked as if he'd stepped straight off the *Spirit of Culver* movie set. Frank wanted to be just like him. It would be glamorous to go a military school, he thought, and the idea of wearing a uniform was more than he could stand.

He asked his uncle to send him to Culver. The 1939 *Life* magazine article observed that military schools once were regarded as the "last resort of desperate parents who could find no other place to send their unruly sons," adding that ". . . today military schools like Culver are essentially good college-preparatory schools."[2] The Colonel was not at the point of desperation with his intractable nephew, but he was well aware that Frank could benefit from the regimentation of military life. Whether he was college material was another matter.

Slover gave his permission for the following autumn. First, though, Frank had to go to Culver's summer school to demonstrate that he could make the grade. Slover urged Culver administrators to be tolerant of his nephew. "I think that Culver is a great institution and I have much faith in what you may do with Frank Batten," he wrote Culver Major J. W. Henderson on July 11, 1940. "It should be remembered that he is only thirteen-and-a-half years old and may require a little extra patience. I am sending you a little box of my Havana cigars, which I hope you may enjoy. S.L.S."[3]

Frank spent eight weeks that summer at Culver, whose 2,000-acre campus is about 100 miles southeast of Chicago. He took classes in arithmetic and reading. His reading speed tripled. He participated in Culver's Naval Camp, sailing Viking sailboats on the north shore of Lake Maxinkuckee. He developed a steady tennis forehand and was an umpire at the National Boys Clay Court Tennis Tournament.

The Colonel, who with Fay had cruised to New York's Thousand Islands Club that summer on their yacht, was pleased to learn that Frank had been accepted for fall admittance to Culver. On August 29, 1940, he wrote to Culver's Henderson, expressing gratitude for the interest shown to his nephew, "who seems greatly improved in health, posture and mind."[4] On September 16, in a brief note to Colonel W. F. Johnston, the sixty-seven-year-old Slover thanked him for "any interest you may take in Frank, who is the same as my son."[5]

Batten entered the ninth grade in the fall of 1940, proudly wearing the brass-buttoned uniform of a Culver plebe. While he saw himself as "plump" and was self-conscious that he was younger than most of his classmates, he had a leg up on many incoming plebes—he'd learned his way around the school over the summer. He also knew how to march and how to do the manual of arms. He wanted to enroll in ROTC but wasn't old enough. His request to be assigned to "C" Company was granted, but the transition to a structured environment was not easy for the boy. By the end of the first term, he was scraping the academic bottom: He flunked social biology and eked out a D+ in English, a C in Latin, and a C+ in algebra.[6] He turned his homework in late, or not at all. He didn't pay attention.

Commander John Roos was Batten's Latin teacher. Roos was infamous for donning full Roman regalia on the Ides of March. As he strode into the classroom, his students would cheer in unison, "Hail Caesar!" Young Batten wasn't particularly impressed with Caesar, or Latin. At one point during the semester, Roos reported Batten to the commandant's office for "trifling" in the classroom. "Today, Mr. Batten spent five minutes or so twirling his overseas cap on the top of a pencil, dropping it every dozen twirls. Then he took to slapping the cap across the knees of the cadet behind him. This, I decided, was too much.

"Perhaps in other situations, he is a charming Virginia gentleman. . . . it may be that there is something peculiar about Latin or about Mr. Roos"—here he referred to himself in the third person—"that affects him in a way that other subjects or instructors do not."[7]

Brain power wasn't the problem, Batten would say decades later. He had little self-confidence, was unfocused and uninterested. "It wasn't," he said, "that I was dumb."

Batten's uncle worried about him. At the beginning of the January 1941 term, Slover called his secretary into his office and dictated a letter to Colonel Johnston, the company tactical officer, with a "few observations about Frank."

As you know, Frank's reactions are slow. While this may not be so good in athletics, I have known such cases of young men to turn it to advantage in practical life later on.

One of Frank's chief difficulties, as you may have observed, I will call timidity—lack of confidence in himself. In ordinary conversation his voice is so low and weak at times it is not audible. I know that he has the strength of voice to make himself heard when he becomes intensely interested or excited, but he is at a distinct disadvantage, I think, in the manner of his speech.

I feel that he should be given some sort of leadership or command to help him. I have noticed that when Frank is with a group of young friends, in the field or on the street, he wants to be well in the rear and I fear would be the last to catch the boat. I should like to see him overcome this and keep his place in the ranks. If you agree with me, what can be done to help him? I often lose sight of the fact that he is not yet fourteen years of age, while I am an old man and probably expect too much of him.[8]

His nephew did little better in the second half of the school year. His English grade dropped from a D+ to a D. After acing the last exam in Mr. Roos's Latin class, his final grade inched up from a C to a C+; algebra stayed the same at C+.

He remained rebellious. On May 14, 1941, just before the end of his first year at Culver, Batten was caught smoking on campus and "denied moving picture privileges" for two weeks.[9] Nine days later, he was kicked out of Culver Military Academy—not for poor grades, recalcitrance, or smoking, but because Batten, age fourteen, had gone to a brothel.

Nearly seventy years later, Batten told of how he and his roommate, Bill Thayer of Charleston, West Virginia, had hatched a plan to end their childhood innocence. "Before we went to sleep, we chatted," Batten said, "and one of the things we chatted about the most was sex. And it just happened that we hadn't had any. And we sort of made a pact. We had one weekend each year that you could take off from school and could be away for two days. And, of course, most people who lived near there went home but we were too far from home. Culver had an inn. We'd just spend the weekend there. We made a pact that we would get laid."[10]

A third classmate, whom Batten and his roommate barely knew, joined them on a Friday night at the venerable Maxinkuckee Inn, and the following afternoon they boarded a passenger train heading north to Logansport, Indiana.

"We got off the train and right next to the train station was a row of about four whorehouses," Batten later recounted. "Culver kids would all joke about the houses. The girls would just be sitting there on the porches. That's where we said we would go. Which we did: We knocked on the door. The madam let us in. We went into the parlor. We were terrified. We sat down and the madam brought four or five girls into the parlor and we just sat there and talked."

This time, Batten was the leader, not a follower. "We didn't know what to do and I remember I was the first to go. I was the first because I was being selfish. I liked the best-looking girl. I said, 'You want to go upstairs?'" Batten declined to elaborate further about the tryst, which he remembered costing him about five dollars, other than to say that it wasn't what he had expected. "I guess I was scared," he allowed.

After their return to Culver, the boy who had joined Frank and his roommate, fearing venereal disease, told the story to the doctor at the infirmary. When word got out, Batten said, the boys were big men on campus—"at least temporarily"—but they got the boot.

Colonel Charles McKinney, the commandant, called Batten into his office. A stern, balding man with rimless spectacles, McKinney saw no humor in the adventure. Talking like a father to a small child, he admonished the teen. "Frank, you're a good boy but you did a bad thing. You have to go home."[11]

Leaving Culver wasn't so bad. Facing his mother, the Colonel, and his aunt Fay in Norfolk, however, was terrifying. It was the longest train ride he'd ever taken. His worst fears never materialized. His mother was convinced that no one had ever told her son the facts of life. Therefore, she said, he was not to blame for his indiscretion. She sent him to the doctor for a lecture. Frank and the doctor thought it was funny.

In the fall of 1941, Batten returned to Culver as an "old man,"

Culver slang for an upperclassman, which gave him license to pick on a plebe like Lucius Parkinson.

"Who won the war?" Batten and his southern classmates demanded of Lucius Parkinson.

"What war?" Parkinson asked.

"The War Between the States."

"The South won!" Parkinson exclaimed, knowing if he gave any other answer he'd get grief from the older students.[12]

Despite the bluster, Batten was on probation and still had little interest in academics and even less self-confidence. By the end of his third semester as a ninth grader, he had barely eked out a C+ in geometry and Cs in English, world history, and a course on Caesar. With an above-average IQ of 116,[13] there was every expectation that Batten should excel. Eventually he did.

Fellow student Lee Winchester, "C" Company's first sergeant and a superb athlete, noticed that Batten was awkward and unsure, and decided to take him under his wing. The Memphis teenager urged the boy to get in shape and to set goals. Batten started running laps and, motivated by Winchester, joined the track team competing in the half-mile run. He came in dead last in every meet.

That didn't matter to Mike Carpenter, Culver's track, cross-country, and boxing coach. He kept after Batten, telling him not to give up. And by repeating a grade, Batten now was the same age as most of the other boys in his class and no longer was playing catch-up with his older peers as he had done in the past. His grade point average jumped from a 1.75 to 2.75. He was soon ranked 69th in a class of 134.

At the end of the school year, the coach held a meeting in the gym to award coveted maroon and white varsity letters. None would go to Batten. But Carpenter did something better: He publicly applauded Batten—who had never won a race and who had never come close to winning one.

Bolstered by the pat on the back, Batten's nascent self-assuredness bloomed. Instead of making a feeble attempt at a task and quitting, he convinced himself that he could improve with effort and tenacious resolve. "That's what the coach was alluding to when he made that little speech," Batten recalled. "He thought I had a lot of guts and didn't give up even when I kept coming in last."[14]

The following school year, Batten earned As and Bs and excelled in English and Spanish. Carpenter persuaded him to try out for Culver's cross-country team, which competed against the likes of the "Fighting Irish" from the University of Notre Dame. During the war, most Indiana high schools and Midwestern prep schools couldn't travel far because of gasoline rationing, so they competed against freshmen from regional colleges.

Batten trailed teammates and competitors in his first cross-country season. With Carpenter's continued encouragement, he pressed on. He had an additional incentive not to finish last: track meets were timed to finish at varsity football games' half-time. The course took runners through the hilly Culver golf course, ending with the best runners crossing the finish line in front of cheering thousands in the football stands. In December 1942, Batten received a varsity letter. Nothing could have made him happier. "What Mike did for me was to give me my first taste of confidence that I could succeed at something, even with limited ability, if I persisted and worked hard," Batten said. "That had a lasting effect on me."

While he was at school, his long-widowed mother married Preston Bass, a Norfolk steamship company shipping agent whom she had dated for several years. Frank liked his stepfather but was never close to him. Bass was "someone who just married my mother," he said. "He knew the situation . . . my uncle was my father and he wasn't displacing him."[15]

Culver faculty were leaving monthly to join the war effort. Germany had swept through most of Europe. Fighting raged in the Pacific. Most Culver students were too young to enlist, but they longed to join the war and envied the few who could sign up. In the meantime, the war sometimes came to them.

On June 15, 1942, ten days after Culver's school year ended, Batten was swimming off the 46th Street beach at his family's Virginia Beach cottage. A two-column convoy of American ships was so close that Batten said he felt he could almost swim out to it. Suddenly, he heard a series of loud thumps and watched, frozen in horror, as the ships were engulfed in flames, victims of a minefield that he later learned had been laid in the ocean by a German U-boat four days earlier.

The 448-ton British trawler *Kingston Ceylonite,* loaned to the United States for escort and mine sweeping, was sunk. Eighteen of its thirty-two crewmembers died. An explosion also rocked the tanker *Robert C. Tuttle,* whose second assistant engineer was blown overboard and drowned. The rest of the forty-eight-man crew abandoned ship in three lifeboats. The blast also disabled the main engines and the steering gear of the tanker *Esso Augusta,* blew off its rudder and stern post, and burst its steam and fuel lines.[16]

Eleven-year-old Robert B. D. Hartman, who is now the historian at Culver, was four blocks away on the same beach visiting relatives when the explosions occurred. The German U-701 was sunk three weeks later by an American A-29 attack bomber armed with depth charges. Its hulk still rests in 110 feet of water east of the Diamond Shoals light tower off the coast of Cape Hatteras, North Carolina.

In his junior year, Batten roomed with Elwood H. "Bud" Hillis, who would go on to serve eight terms as a congressman from Indiana's Fifth District. They had a third-floor corner room with two windows and good views. With the addition of bedspreads and carpeting, the room was so homey and comfortable that the duty officer told the boys it looked like a country club. Hillis remembered Batten, by then a model student, as quiet and even-tempered. As a company sergeant, Hillis recalled, Batten counseled a boy who wanted to run away.[17]

One icy December night, Batten was studying at his desk, which faced the window, when he motioned to his roommate to look outside. A young cadet, wearing an overcoat and with a bag slung over his shoulder, was leaving the grounds. Hillis ran down the stairs and out the door. It was a plebe from his own unit, and he was running away from Culver ten days before Christmas break. Hillis convinced him to come back to the room to talk. Batten, a company sergeant, advised the boy, perhaps remembering his own shaky first year.

"Look, you may not be happy here but don't do a foolish thing like this," Batten said. "Wait until the holiday break and go home and tell your parents how you feel. Then make a family decision."

The boy nodded and said he would. The homesick classmate had no food and little money, and the nearest bus service was ten miles away. He probably would have tried to hitchhike but there was not much traffic because of gasoline rationing. He stayed at Culver until Christmas vacation. He did not come back.

For Batten, one memory of his Culver days stood out in particular.

His aunt, uncle, and mother were in the school's football stadium watching him participate in the manual of arms competition held at the close of his junior year. The best candidate from each military organization in the regiment's nine units—four infantry, band, two cavalry troops, and two batteries of artillery—formed in front of the Riding Hall. In the drill-down, Batten took top honors. It was the most pride he'd ever seen his uncle express.

Batten, with one more year of high school, was one of Culver's top cadets. He has "a good mind and an unusual faculty of expression," wrote school counselor J. Hobart Tucker. Batten, he added, was "extremely popular and an excellent officer, and by his example is contributing in a major way to a really successful year not only for 'C' Company but for the entire Corps."[18] Batten was a member of the Cadet Club, an organization of cadet captains; the Honor Council; and the Honor Guard. He didn't join the campus newspaper staff because he didn't think he had much literary talent and there was no room for it in his schedule, anyway. In addition to track and cross-country, the 6-foot, 145-pound teenager also learned to box in his senior year, although he said he was no more than a "punching bag for the good guys." Coach Carpenter told him at graduation that of all the sports Batten had tried, boxing was the one for which he had the most talent and should have started earlier.

Batten was selected as one of seven company commanders in his senior year. Except for a rotating battalion commander, the only higher rank than company commander was the regimental commander, who led the entire corps of cadets. His roommate, Lucius Parkinson, whom Batten had picked on as a plebe, held that position.

Parkinson remembered Batten as "very blond" and "very hand-some." Parkinson said while his friend and roommate didn't have a whole lot of natural talent, he worked hard and he was honest. Parkinson described Batten as a private, quiet person, blessed with a good sense of humor and a gift for telling a story. He and Warren Ornstein, another classmate, gave Batten the moniker "Nok," which they said Batten disliked immensely.

Batten graduated from Culver on June 5, 1945, with honors in military science. He ranked twenty-seventh in a class of 161.[19] His class photo is that of a serious teenager with a thin face, intense eyes, a high forehead, and wavy strawberry blond hair.

He led his troops to win the Austin Trophy, awarded to the corps' best infantry company, in the 1945 competition. The achievement was no surprise to John R. Mars, an instructor at Culver and its superintendent from 1976 to 1982. Mars regarded Batten as a cadet who had leadership "exuding from every pore of his body." Some leaders are bullies and take advantage of their position, he said, but that wasn't Batten's style. He had character. He led by example. "It's a compliment if you can get people under you to want to follow without having to yell, as he did," Mars said.[20]

Batten was strict with the more than seventy cadets in "C" Company. His leadership style was hardnosed and firm. "Some resented his disciplinary actions," Parkinson believed, "and he won the Austin at the expense of his own popularity. He didn't want to compromise standards he had set up in his own head. I think he alienated some people in the process."

Culver was the school closest to his heart, Batten said, because it influenced him "by far" more than any other. He learned to believe in himself there. He developed leadership and decision-making skills. He found he had a strong desire to succeed.

"If I had not been motivated by several other students to want to be a leader," he said, "and if I had not stuck my neck out to seek leadership, I would not have been put in a position to experience leadership."

His first cash gift to Culver was in 1953. "After a couple of years in the service and many years in school, I am finally earning a living. Although I am a little late, I would like to make a donation to the Culver chapel and am enclosing a check for $500."[21] More — much more — would follow.

From 1985 to 2002, he served as a member of the Culver Educational Foundation Board of Trustees. In 1999, Culver created the Batten Scholarship with a series of gifts from Frank Batten totaling $11.1 million. The Batten Scholarship is modeled after the University of North Carolina's Morehead Scholarship program, the first non-athletic, merit-based scholarship, itself patterned after Oxford University's Rhodes Scholarship. The full ride is offered to six incoming students, and covers tuition, room and board, fees, uniforms, and books, as well as the cost of an off-site summer study program.

In 2003, Batten donated an additional $20.8 million to Culver, the largest single gift to the school and at the time the largest single contribution to any secondary private school in the country. Half of the gift was designated to enhance the Batten Scholarship program. The remainder endowed faculty development, curriculum improvements, and acquisition of new educational technologies. In the fall of 2008, Batten and his wife committed to another $20 million endowment fund to establish a Batten Fellows program for faculty pay. They also said they'd match dollar-for-dollar all endowment gifts paid in cash through January 31, 2010, for Culver's endowment, up to $50 million. The entire amount was raised, said Head of Schools John Buxton. The Battens' gifts to Culver totaled $104 million. The couple were named the 2010 recipients of the Seymour Preston Award from the Council for Advancement and Support of Education.

Batten has given hundreds of millions of dollars to education— high schools, colleges, and universities. "Education is the best means to perpetuate the kind of society we have, in which there is a large scale of opportunities for people of all status to make headway in life and to advance with their ambitions," he said. "I believe the most important factor in preserving a free society is to have an open society where people of all kinds of means can find opportunity and take advantage of it. And I believe that education provides the fuel that makes this fluid society work."

The alternative, he explained, is a "frozen society" in which only the privileged few, born into wealth or opportunity, have access to education and leadership positions.[22] His years at Culver made him gratefully aware of the value of that access. Batten said he could not imagine a better way to teach leadership than the school's system. It helped him develop integrity and self-esteem. He sought his first major challenges—and savored his first victories.

4 "Growth through Change"

MERCHANT MARINE AND THE
UNIVERSITY OF VIRGINIA

ULVER'S ACADEMIC office had hoped that Batten would go directly to college after graduation. He wanted to go to war. "The attitude during World War II was that a lot of people really wanted to go to war and I was one of them," he said. "I felt that it was the honorable thing to do and the proper thing to do."[1]

After the Normandy invasion, he and roommate Lucius Parkinson, who were both senior ROTC leaders, collaborated on a letter to General George S. Patton somewhat facetiously complimenting him on his tactics. "We appreciate it and hope to be there" before the war is over, they wrote, mailing the letter to Patton in care of the U.S. Third Army, France. To their surprise, the two young men received a reply "thanking them for their concern."

The Colonel encouraged Batten to attend the U.S. Naval Academy because it would keep him away from the conflict, and "out of the shooting." Slover had considerable political influence and was certain he could get his nephew an appointment. It didn't hurt that a former managing editor for the *Virginian-Pilot* was the district congressman.

Batten had no interest in getting an appointment with such pull. And he didn't want to escape the fighting. After spending five years at a military prep school, he had learned to look like a soldier, think like a soldier, and act like a soldier. Now he wanted to be one.

By the time Batten graduated from Culver in June 1945, the fighting in Europe was over, and war in the Pacific was nearing an end. Navy Officer Candidate School, his first choice, had achieved its quota. The Army and Air Corps officer training programs also were filled. The only option was the U.S. Merchant Marine Academy's

OCS. At least Batten would be at sea, which he loved. He had grown up on the water and had been around boats all his life.

Two weeks after leaving Culver, Batten said good-bye to his family, climbed aboard a Norfolk & Western Railway train at Norfolk's Union Depot, and began his journey to Kings Point, New York. The train slowly pulled out of the station, today the site of a baseball stadium where the Norfolk Tides—affiliated with the New York Mets from 1969 to 2006 and as the Baltimore Orioles' Triple A farm team since 2007—plays its home games. Passenger cars were jammed with servicemen and -women heading home on leave or traveling between duty stations. It wasn't easy for anyone to get a reserved seat, but Colonel Slover was one of the railroad's directors. His nephew had managed to get a reservation.

The academy on Long Island's North Shore had been dedicated two years earlier by President Roosevelt, who'd said it would serve the Merchant Marine "as West Point serves the Army and Annapolis the Navy."[2] Batten arrived on June 20, 1945, anticipating three months of basic training at Kings Point and up to a year at sea before returning to the academy for six additional months of classroom instruction. He'd then be commissioned as an officer.

He and his fellow midshipmen were exhilarated by Germany's defeat. They expected that the next big thrust would be an invasion of Japan. On August 6, Batten was in his dormitory just before dinner when he heard a radio report that the United States had dropped an atomic bomb on Hiroshima, Japan. Batten jumped down from his top bunk to catch details of the devastation. It was difficult to comprehend a nuclear weapon—nicknamed "Little Boy"—which was 2,000 times more powerful than the largest conventional bomb ever used. The stunned midshipmen cheered. The war appeared to be over.

The academy celebrated by giving midshipmen a two-day pass. Batten traveled to his Virginia home by rail, this time without reserved seating. He stood for nearly the entire trip alongside other servicemen who were trying to get home, too. A dozen hours after leaving New York, Batten arrived in Norfolk by way of Petersburg,

Virginia, where he got off the train and hitchhiked the remaining seventy-five miles. When Batten returned to New York, he was ordered to sea duty—the first of several trips across the Atlantic to transport fresh troops to Europe and to bring war-weary American soldiers home. Batten and five other midshipmen joined the crew of the *John Ericsson,* a 609-foot troop transport bound for London. It had started service in the late 1920s as an ocean liner for the Swedish-America line Kungsholm, and had been sold to the U.S. War Shipping Administration in 1942.[3]

That fall and winter, vicious storms churned the North Atlantic and heaved tons of water over the ship. With waves washing over its bow, troops clung to lifelines while moving topside. Nearly everyone around him was seasick, but Batten wasn't. As a child learning to sail, he had embraced the challenge of coping with the elements. Later in life as a competitive sailor he'd prefer sailing when there was a brisk breeze and stiff waves.

When he was in port and off duty, Batten was drawn to New York's night life. One evening, he dropped by a Greenwich Village nightclub jammed with revelers. When the club closed in the early morning, he escorted a young woman home on the subway. After seeing her to her door, he headed back to the ship. Plunking a token in the turnstile, Batten impatiently waited for the next train. When it arrived, he wearily dropped into a seat, leaned his head against the window, and fell fast asleep. He rode back and forth on the subway line until a conductor woke him after daybreak.

One of Batten's most vivid memories of his two years in the Merchant Marine was coming face-to-face with racism. He and an academy classmate asked to be assigned to the same merchant ship. They both were posted to the *John Ericsson,* Batten for the second time, as it set sail for Germany carrying a load of Army nurses to Bremerhaven, a German industrial port city on the Weser River near the North Sea. Batten, three other midshipmen, and four nurses celebrated New Year's Eve on the crossing, partying throughout the night, out of sight of officers three decks above them.

On arriving in Bremerhaven, then called Wesermunde, they

were stunned to see a city that had been nearly obliterated in the war. In twenty minutes on a single day, more than 600 people had been killed, 1,100 injured, 30,000 left homeless, and more than 2,000 buildings destroyed.[4] Batten stepped ashore into a sea of rubble.

After an eight-hour duty shift, Batten and a buddy went to the Officers' Club, signed in, and headed to the bar. After a few drinks they heard men arguing at the entrance of the club and went to check it out. A white southern Army major was berating a black lieutenant for attempting to come into the club. "My friend and I being eighteen-year-olds and thinking we were smarter than we were, we got in the middle of the argument on the side of the lieutenant," Batten remembered. "We were incensed. We thought it was bad to kick this guy out. He was an officer and it seemed to us that a black officer had just as much the right to be there as the white officers." The military police were called. Batten, his friend, and a couple of other men who had sided with the ostracized soldier were tossed out of the club.

It was out of the ordinary for a white southerner to publicly take a stand against racial indignity and injustice. Batten's own past made it a remarkable moment. His family had employed black servants. People of color didn't live in his neighborhood; they came there to work. Their children didn't go to school or play there. Like other southern states, his was deeply segregated; the overwhelming belief among whites was that segregation was acceptable.

That night in Germany wasn't the first time he experienced bigotry; that occurred when he was eight or nine years old. A black child, not more than ten, had pedaled by Batten's home on his bicycle. Batten and three or four other kids started yelling at the boy, demanding that he get out of the neighborhood because he didn't belong there.

Mattu Collette, Colonel Slover's black driver and all-around handyman, heard Batten rebuke the child. Hurt and angry, Collette told him, "You ought not to do that, that's wrong!" The boy had as much right to be on that street as Frank did, Collette said.

Batten loved Mattu, and he had disappointed him. "I expect," he said years later, "that's the first time I ever confronted the idea of race relations." Those two incidents—being admonished by a black man he cared for, and witnessing the unfairness of a black American officer being barred from an all-white military club in a foreign city—would foreshadow an episode in Batten's later life in which he took a stand that would define him.

The Merchant Marine was a good experience. It reinforced Batten's love of the ocean. He also learned a thing or two about leadership. Some of his bosses had been eager to help him and his fellow midshipmen grow and learn. Others could not have cared less.

On one Atlantic crossing, Batten was assigned to a 459-foot-long C2 cargo ship. Without first asking permission, he went on the ship's bridge and retrieved the sextant from its cabinet to take a navigation sighting. Furious that Batten hadn't put the instrument back exactly the way he'd found it, the captain ordered him to "stay the hell off the bridge" for the rest of the voyage. Batten was made the ship's "captain of the dogs" and was put in charge of feeding and cleaning up after some twenty canines in one of the five holds.

Being at sea gave Batten plenty of time to think about his future. While Colonel Slover never pressured him to join his newspapers, it was no secret that he hoped his nephew would follow in his footsteps. Batten eventually recognized that nobody was going to offer him a better opportunity than his uncle. He also became more and more interested in public affairs. What better way to learn what was going on across the ocean, in Washington, or in his own backyard than by getting the information first-hand at his uncle's newspapers?

His only hesitation arose from his uncle's high expectations. Batten planned to go to college first but he wasn't sanguine about his ability to succeed at the newspapers. "I didn't know if I was up to it," he said.

In December 1946, he left the Merchant Marine Academy for civilian schooling. He applied to the University of Virginia, where most of his friends were bound, and the following February entered the school with enough credits from the Merchant Marine Academy to qualify as a second-semester freshman. He also signed up for ROTC.

Of all Batten's educational experiences, U.Va. would prove the least challenging. Core subjects were easy for him, not because he was particularly smart, he said, but because at the time the school's standards were low. He took several courses that he judged equivalent to classes he'd had at Culver Military Academy three years earlier.

Having decided to go into business with his uncle, Batten thought economics would be the most useful course of study. He found the subject "incredibly dull." Two instructors did leave a lasting impression on Batten, including economics professor David McCord Wright. The author of nine books, Wright went on to teach at other unversities, including Oxford, and his scholarship helped shape Batten's economic philosophy. Students remembered Wright's refrain: "Growth comes through change and causes change." It would become an axiom for Batten as he later expanded his uncle's company.

An English professor taught Batten the lifelong value of writing clearly—to keep language simple and straightforward. He did it by humiliating his students. He'd pick out papers written for class and ridicule them as he read them aloud. "I mean, brutally ridiculed them," Batten remembered, grimacing. Not a naturally gifted writer, Batten was the subject of the professor's taunting more times than he'd have liked, but he learned to write succinctly and well.

The most valuable product of his U.Va. experience was lasting friendships at Delta Kappa Epsilon, U.Va.'s first fraternity and the oldest in Virginia, whose national roster claims such notables as presidents Teddy Roosevelt, Gerald Ford, and both George Bushes. Beer and whiskey bottles littered the yard of the Georgian-style DKE house, and a keg of brew anchored the front porch. The basement, which doubled as a party room, was coated with a thick layer of sawdust so when anyone passed out he wouldn't kill himself, said Batten, who was the house's assistant manager. Batten more than held his own when it came to drinking, poker, and partying, said Henry Burnett, Batten's roommate in his last year at U.Va., but he was more circumspect and serious than most of his fraternity brothers

—so much so that some called him "Mother Batten." Other friends christened him "Jelly" because of his penchant for grape jelly.

During summer vacations, Batten worked at his uncle's newspapers as a copy boy and reporter. Carefree summer nights were spent at his mother and stepfather's Virginia Beach oceanfront cottage, sunbathing with friends by day and dancing in the evenings to the beat of big bands like Glenn Miller or Tommy Dorsey at the Surf Beach Club and the Cavalier Hotel's beach club.

In his final year at U.Va., Batten moved out of the DKE house to room with Burnett, then in his last year at U.Va. Law School, and law student Ken McElwain, who were renting from a professor. It was a one-room apartment on the second floor of a garage with a bath and a screened-in porch. Batten slept on the porch. When the weather turned frosty, he stayed warm by burrowing under piles of down comforters. "His rise to fame I attribute to the toughness of him having to spend the entire winter on that screened-in porch," Burnett later joked.[5]

Batten graduated in the spring of 1950. He skipped commencement and on June 7 set off on a three-month tour of Europe, a graduation gift from his family. With him was his friend St. John Bain, newly graduated from the Massachusetts Institute of Technology. They made the week-long passage on the *Nieuw Amsterdam,* a 36,600-ton Holland-America ocean liner that had been restored to its original art deco grandeur after service as a British troop ship during the war.

As the *Nieuw Amsterdam* sailed out of New York harbor, Bain and Batten went down to the lounge for a drink. A serious student, Bain had always stayed away from the beer and bourbon, opting instead for ginger ale. "Frank ordered a scotch. I ordered my ginger ale," Bain recalled. "Frank looked at the ginger ale and said in amazement, 'Saint, they're serving Johnnie Walker Black for twenty-five cents and ginger ale for twenty-five cents and you're drinking ginger ale?'" Bain switched to scotch.[6]

Highlights of the summer included time spent in Antibes with Elizabeth Taylor, then eighteen years old and honeymooning with her husband Nicky Hilton, heir to the Hilton hotel chain. The new-lyweds were staying at the luxurious white-walled Hôtel du Cap at Eden Roc built on a 22-acre peninsula jutting into the Mediterra-nean. With her husband holed up nights in the Monte Carlo casino and sleeping during the day, Taylor was looking for company. Batten and Bain were at a small hotel nearby, but for a dollar, American vet-erans could get into the beach club at the ritzy hotel, the model for the Hôtel des Étrangers in F. Scott Fitzgerald's *Tender Is the Night.* Taylor didn't talk about Hollywood and was like any other teenage girl, Batten said—except that she was famous, beautiful, and alone.

In Oberammergau, Germany, Batten and Bain spent the night in jail—the only place with room, according to a policeman they en-countered when they arrived in the middle of the night. The beds were clean. And hard.

In England, the last stop on their European pilgrimage, they met Nancy Witcher Langhorne, better known as Lady Astor, to whom they had a letter of introduction. A native of Danville, Virginia, Lady Astor went to school with Bain's grandmother and great-aunt. Bat-ten's mother was friends with one of the socialite's four sisters. Stun-ningly beautiful, Langhorne had married in New York, divorced, and moved to England where she wed Waldorf Astor in the spring of 1906. By 1919 she had been elected to the House of Commons as the first woman to hold a seat in Parliament.

Batten and Bain telephoned her at her London flat and made plans to meet the next day. "Frank and I showed up at noon in our clean khakis," Bain recalled. Lady Astor admonished them after learning that the two had been in London earlier that summer. "You ninnies," scolded the unconventional seventy-one-year-old. "I have an annual party and I could have introduced you to the king and queen." She invited the pair to her summer house near Sandwich, a medieval town in Kent, not far from the famed White Cliffs of Dover.

After seeing the local sights through the eyes of one of England's most celebrated aristocrats, Batten and Bain returned to London. Lady Astor told them to plan on visiting Windsor Castle where she'd arrange for them to view its private rooms. The night before the tour, she telephoned them in their London hotel room. "I hope you don't mind," she trilled. "I've arranged for some other people to go with you—Mr. and Mrs. John D. Rockefeller III and his family."

They were to meet the Rockefellers in front of Claridges Hotel at 9 a.m. Wanting to make a good impression, the young men rented a Rolls Royce, with a driver. Promptly at 9, Rockefeller pulled up in front of the hotel in an MG.

"Looks like you have a little more room than we do," he observed. "Could you accommodate my son Jay and his friend?" After touring Windsor and Eton and motoring through the English countryside, the Rolls and the MG stopped at an inn for lunch. Batten offered to pick up the tab. "We'll go Dutch for lunch, right?" Rockefeller replied, and paid for his own family's meal.

5 Heir Apparent

SAMUEL SLOVER was seventy-seven years old when his nephew graduated from the University of Virginia. He didn't know how many more years he'd be able to continue working, and he was anxious for his nephew to begin learning the newspaper business and eventually run the company. Neither Batten's mother nor his aunt was interested in a career outside the home. Not many women worked for newspapers anyway, and the few who did tended to be reporters, not CEOs. Batten was the only member of the immediate family who could take over the family business.

As a little boy, Frank had been excited when a Linotype operator set his name in hot lead type. In the summer of 1941, when he was fourteen, he had worked as a copy boy in the advertising department, delivering advertising proofs to downtown Norfolk businesses on foot or by streetcar—though even at that age, he was conscious that other employees might think: "There's a kid with a silver spoon in his mouth." As he grew older, Colonel Slover had started grooming his nephew to run the company by giving him experience in various newspaper departments.

The newsroom was his favorite. Newspapers were loud, dirty, and exciting. Like the set of the 1931 newspaper movie *The Front Page,* reporters' desks groaned under mountains of yellowing newspapers, notebooks, unwashed coffee mugs, glue pots, green eyeshades, and overflowing ashtrays. A bottle of whiskey was hidden in more than one drawer. The Associated Press teletype machines spat out news reports from around the world. The rewrite man, cradling a telephone handset on his shoulder, took dictation from newsmen calling in stories from phone booths. As deadline approached, the bustle turned to frenzy. Editors yelled to reporters that they needed copy, then made edits and tossed the marked-up stories in an out-basket, where they were snatched up by a copy boy for the copy desk to edit again and add headlines. The stories were then rushed to the composing room, where compositors sat at Linotype machines, ceiling-high mechanical behemoths. With each tap of the machine's keyboard, a brass mold of a letter dropped into a narrow groove the same width as a newspaper column. Once a line was filled, molten metal from a 540-degree melting pot flowed through the machine into tiny molds for each line of type. Lines of type, or "slugs," were then pushed into a metal galley. It was hot, loud, dirty work.

More steps followed—to the engraving, makeup, and stereotype departments—before finished metal plates, a mirror-image of each page, rendered in lead, were attached to enormous cylinders on presses two stories high, loaded with five-mile-long rolls of news-print, each weighing three-quarters of a ton. With a deafening roar the rolling presses transformed the newsprint to a black and white blur; other machines cut and folded the papers, which chugged along a conveyer to the mailroom. Within hours, paperboys fetched bundles of newspapers and hurled the latest news onto subscribers' porches.

In August 1947, Batten wrote his first bylined story: he drove his 1941 Oldsmobile to fourteen garages and asked mechanics at each for an annual safety inspection. Seven of the stations were too busy to look under the hood or anywhere else. Three garages gave the Olds a thumbs-up and issued an inspection sticker. Four inspectors rejected the car pending repairs that ranged from $1.40 to $37.80. The following day, the *Ledger-Dispatch* printed an editorial that was longer than Batten's news story. It called on the state Division of Motor Vehicles to "inspect its designated inspectors."

The next summer, Batten was a full-fledged journalist for the *Ledger-Dispatch*'s Virginia Beach office. Decades later, the ocean-front community would be the commonwealth's largest city with a population of more than 440,000; in the late 1940s it was home to just a tenth as many souls. William M. Snider was the *Ledger*'s only full-time reporter there. He was bureau chief, too, "being that he was the chief," Batten later observed, "of himself."

Batten wrote features about celebrities visiting Virginia Beach, such as Betty Smith, author of *A Tree Grows in Brooklyn,* and the Right Reverend Henry St. George Tucker, retired presiding bishop of the Episcopal Church of the United States, who reminisced about growing up on the poor side of Norfolk. Batten had been raised on one side of the Hague, a creek in downtown Norfolk, and Tucker, the oldest of thirteen children, had spent his youth on the other side of the water. Tucker lived in a white slum with dilapidated housing, Batten remembered. "The kids there were really tough. Any kid from our side of the Hague who ventured over there would get beat up. They were mean sons of bitches."

Tucker testified in the interview with Batten to that view—he confessed that as a child he had pushed a boy from Batten's side of the creek off a small boat and into the Hague. The *Ledger* editor was tickled with the exchange and impressed that the young reporter had gotten the bishop to tell the story.

Batten considered a career in the newsroom, but knew his uncle saw him as an eventual publisher. Despite the Colonel's eagerness, Batten wasn't ready to take up the family business. First, he told his uncle, he wanted to go to Harvard Business School.

Slover was lukewarm to the idea and did his best to persuade his nephew that he didn't need a graduate degree. One of the Colonel's close friends, Homer L. Ferguson, was president of Virginia's Newport News Shipbuilding and Drydock Company, the largest privately owned shipyard in the country. He urged Slover to back off. Don't talk him out of it, he advised. Slover, who had tremendous respect for Ferguson, heeded his advice.

Batten enrolled at Harvard in the autumn of 1950. Once classes started, there were times when he wondered whether he had made the right decision. Was he in over his head? His cousin Fay Martin Chandler and her husband, Alfred, were living in nearby Brookline, Massachusetts, while Alfred worked on his Ph.D. and taught at both Harvard and MIT. Batten occasionally went to their home for dinner and confided in Fay that he was "feeling really swamped," a development he hadn't expected. The business school students had been given massive reading assignments, and he was struggling to keep up.

Despite his worry, Fay, named after her aunt Fay Slover, knew her cousin would succeed, that he wouldn't go home "with his tail between his legs" after Slover had been against him going to Harvard. "He began to catch on that they don't expect you to know everything —you have to learn what's important," Chandler said later. Batten eventually prioritized his assignments and settled in.

Between the first and second years of his MBA program, Batten worked again for his uncle. He sold advertising space in the newspapers, usually calling on stores in downtown Norfolk. Sometimes he'd tag along with the advertising sales manager on his stop at the paper's largest advertiser, Sears, Roebuck and Co. The newspaper's retail sales manager came up with a plan to sell a "double truck," or centerfold for newspaper advertising. The twin pages were divided into sixteen ads. Batten and sales rep Ernest L. Posey Jr., whom Batten called a great salesman who loved his job, were each to peddle eight ads. "Well, he got started the day before me and sold the eight ads on the outside of the pages. I was left with the eight ads on the inside, which was not as good," Batten remembered. "It was typical of Posey. It was a joke between us and people kidded me because I had to work a lot harder to sell my eight."

At Harvard, Batten kept details about his personal life to himself. "You could room with him and still not know a lot about him," recalled roommate Robert R. Fair.[1] He didn't talk much about Culver or his family, said Frank Thompson, another Harvard roommate. He knew Batten planned to go into the newspaper business, but Thompson had no idea that his family was wealthy. "He never, *never*, talked about it."[2]

Unlike many of his classmates, Batten knew exactly where he would be working after graduation. Harvard's case study method was particularly relevant because it used real-life business situations that he was likely to confront almost immediately at his uncle's newspapers. As Harvard promised, it provided insights into how to "grapple with exactly the kinds of decisions and dilemmas managers confront every day." And with those decision-making skills came the leadership know-how that Batten sought.

One unidentified case study was easily recognized by Batten as Goss International, a manufacturer of newspaper presses that had been around since 1885. "Were you to read the case, you'd think the company doesn't have many years left because the newspaper business was going to fail," Batten said.[3] "All the trends, after World War II, were against newspapers. Radio was gaining strength, television was about to happen." Following the exam about the case, Batten said a couple of his classmates questioned him about why he would even consider going into the newspaper business.

One Harvard professor taught him a lesson he would not forget. Batten had done well throughout the semester in a marketing class. On the day of the final exam, he fell sick with a high fever. He took the exam anyway, penning nearly incoherent answers. After the exam, he was diagnosed with chicken pox and admitted to the hospital. Following his discharge a week later, Batten went to the professor, knowing that he had done poorly on the final. "I begged him to let me take the exam over. He said, 'You'll have to make up the grade in the second semester.'" Batten was furious. "I thought he was a prick," he said. "That was the only bad grade I'd gotten." Years later, Batten understood what the professor might have been trying to teach him—that there always will be unfortunate circumstances in business. You simply have to learn to cope with them.

Culver had taught Batten to believe in himself. It gave him leadership experience. Harvard provided him with the technical skills to be a leader in business—to think strategically and to make tough decisions. He'd held his own with a lot of very bright men, many of whom had had significant business experience.

"Solve problems, make decisions, set up priorities; those are the main things I got at Harvard . . . and confidence," Batten said. "I don't think I could have survived without having that experience. Survive is a big word, but I wouldn't have handled it as well as I did." That confidence would quickly be called upon.

Slover, in his later years, had trimmed his presence at Norfolk

Newspapers, eventually serving only in an advisory role as board chairman. Paul Huber was his right-hand man, to whom, with Frederick Lewis, Slover had sold a majority of *Ledger* stock in 1930. A respected leader, Huber had worked his way up from general manager to publisher and president. When Norfolk Newspapers acquired Norfolk radio station WTAR, he also became its president, and later its chairman.

Huber died unexpectedly in September 1946. It was a blow to the Colonel, who saw Huber as "an executive of superb ability, and as a man of fine human traits and of deep inner strength." Before his death, Huber had willed voting control of his stock to Slover. With both his own stock and Huber's, Slover again commanded the newspapers. It was not a responsibility he wanted to assume at his age, but he felt it necessary because he didn't believe Lewis was capable of running the business. Responsibility for operating the papers was turned over, ironically, to Henry S. Lewis, Frederick's nephew and the company's secretary and assistant treasurer. The enraged elder Lewis regarded his nephew as a traitor. While Henry Lewis wasn't a strong leader, he was the most broadly experienced manager at the newspapers.[4]

Six years after Huber's death, with a prestigious Harvard MBA under his belt, Batten set out to learn the newspaper business full-time under his uncle's tutelage. As he did, Slover, now an octogenarian, began to devise a way for his nephew to gain control of the company.

At the age of twenty-five, Batten already owned a substantial amount of stock that the Colonel had given to him as a child. Slover also arranged to have his estate sell his nephew his remaining stock after his death on generous terms similar to those he'd offered the *Ledger* executives years earlier.

As a result of the newspapers' merger in 1933, the *Ledger-Dispatch*'s stockholders held two-thirds of the 15,000 shares of stock in Norfolk Newspapers, and *Pilot* shareholders owned the remaining third. No one, however, would hold a controlling interest in the *Ledger-Dispatch*'s share of stock once the Colonel died. An agreement was made to trade the Slovers' Richmond Newspapers stock to the Frederick Lewis family for the Lewis family's *Ledger-Dispatch* stock, the trade to take place after the Colonel's death. The Norfolk newspapers would then be fully controlled by the Slover family, with his widow and nephew holding the majority of the stock.

With the company's future settled, for the next two years Batten received a hands-on introduction to the advertising, circulation, and promotions departments at both Norfolk papers. He watched and listened, and what he saw was a company that was making money but lacked direction. He believed that the organization under Henry Lewis had no momentum, no dynamism. There also was no cooperation between offices, no unified drive. Departments were fiefdoms led by managers who should have retired years earlier. Batten shared his concerns with his uncle, who agreed with him; Lewis was coasting, and key managers had to step aside. Slover urged the newspapers' board of directors to set up a committee to identify improvements.

As one of the committee members, Batten set out to modernize the newspapers' management structure. Change was essential, Batten believed, to upgrade the quality of the staff, particularly in the newsroom and advertising departments. Norfolk Newspapers Inc. needed better-educated employees who brought a fresh perspective to a constantly evolving business. He was impatient to get things moving. Over the years, he considered the best bit of business advice he received from his uncle was "Keep your bowels loose." In other words, stay flexible, ready, and fast.

In October 1954, publisher Henry Lewis died with no obvious successor. Slover, who had been disconnected from day-to-day operations for years, agonized over who would replace Lewis. Batten and Paul Huber Jr. were the only internal candidates Slover found even remotely acceptable. Both were young men, military veterans who had studied economics in college. Both had turned in good service to the newspapers, Huber for five years longer than Batten. Until one or both young men were better qualified to run the company, Slover considered bringing in his friend John D. Wise, general manager of the Richmond dailies, to operate the newspapers.

Kaufman, Slover's lawyer, friend, and confidant, strongly urged Slover to appoint Batten to the top job. A short, gracious man, Kaufman had a rare combination of brilliance and practicality, good judgment and sound instincts when it came to both people and business. After several conversations with Kaufman, Slover talked at length with his nephew. Though Batten was less experienced than Huber, Slover thought it prudent to place him in a position of authority while he was able to advise him. He concluded that he should put his nephew in control immediately, rather than someone from the outside who'd require a long-term commitment.

On October 27, 1954, Slover named his nephew publisher of the *Virginian-Pilot* and *Ledger-Dispatch*.[5] Five days later, vice president of WTAR Radio-TV Corporation was added to his title. Batten was twenty-seven. Huber, thirty-three, was appointed president. Batten was charged with running news, circulation, advertising, and public relations, the departments that he and his uncle deemed most critical to the company's future success. Huber had responsibility for the business office, production, personnel, and employee relations. It was two-headed leadership that depended on Batten and Huber getting along, which they did.

Batten not only was young, he was unseasoned, unknown, and despite his strides in recent years, unsure of himself. Outwardly at least, he was accepted by the much older men ("they were all men," he said) who now reported to him. There had not been a lot of respect for Henry Lewis, and Batten guessed they'd preferred "this young guy they knew" to having someone brought in from the outside whom they didn't know.

Batten was well aware that his uncle provided him with a break that few ever got—to reach the top of an influential and powerful business so young, without a struggle to get there. But he would make the most of his opportunity, growing the privately held company into a media powerhouse.

"In fact," Batten said, "I think I even made more than the most of it."

6 Taking Charge

THE NEW PUBLISHER

BATTEN LEFT THE familiar hubbub of the newspapers' advertising department and moved to the quiet inner sanctum of his uncle's former office. He sat behind a rectangular, glass-top mahogany table facing his guests. A massive roll-top desk was at his back. From his third-floor corner office, he could see the sprawl of downtown Norfolk with its Georgian and Federal period houses, the Hague Yacht Basin, and beyond, the Elizabeth River. A handful of high-rises, most from early in the century, formed the city's compact skyline.

Batten had been preparing for the challenge of his new position for years but feared he would not be up to it. He was in awe of his uncle and pushed himself to meet his exacting standards. "I'd think: 'How can I follow him?'"

In his younger days, his lack of confidence had made him more of a follower than a leader. Now that he had taken over as publisher, he knew that a lot of people expected him to fail. "Not because of who I was," he said, "but they couldn't understand the idea of a twenty-seven-year-old with no experience becoming publisher and succeeding." He struggled. As publisher, he was called on to handle dicey situations that his uncle in his waning years had ignored or had failed to notice. He was overwhelmed, finding it difficult to prioritize a multitude of tasks, as he had done at Harvard. He slept poorly.

For guidance, he turned to mentors like *Virginian-Pilot* associate editor Harold G. Sugg, for whom he created a position of assistant to the publisher, and attorney Charles Kaufman, who had advised Colonel Slover. The neophyte publisher often walked the several blocks to Kaufman's downtown law firm to discuss sensitive matters that he could not share with office colleagues. Batten's closest counselor, in both legal and business matters, Kaufman was in Batten's view "one of the best business minds of anybody I've known." Batten, who still lived with the Slovers, also constantly sought the Colonel's advice. Slover seldom expressed his opinion, except when his nephew asked for it or wanted to hash out a plan or problem.

Batten relied on business books as well, particularly Peter Drucker's *The Practice of Management*, published in 1954. The book posed three questions for leaders to ask themselves: What is our business? Who is our customer? What does our customer consider valuable?[1] Batten read the book no fewer than five times over the next dozen years, as well as many of the economist's other works, devouring his management-by-objective theories and asking the same three questions of his senior managers. Drucker's theories about motivating, communicating, and developing people became part of Batten's management mantra for the rest of his career.

Other lessons weren't as easily grasped. Batten was soft on people who were poor performers, compensating for them or managing around them. This ran counter to Drucker, who held that managers should be treated humanely but should never be left in a position of influence once the decision had been made that they were unable to learn or change. "I had a view I ought to be very tolerant," Batten said. "I intended to go the last mile in trying to save them." Over time, Drucker's words convinced him he was not being humane at all—the poor performer was harming a lot of other people in the organization, as well as the company itself.

Retirement at the newspapers was rarely considered and wasn't mandatory. Often, employees wouldn't stop working until they were either too sick to push a pencil or dropped dead at their desks. A pension plan had been in place prior to Batten's ascendancy, but few had chosen to take advantage of it. Those who did typically were printers and pressmen. Batten instituted a policy that required all managers to retire at the age of sixty-five.

The new policy was met with some resistance among the old guard. While the newspapers lost valuable institutional knowledge, the policy created movement within the ranks. With the departure of an aging workforce, new opportunities opened to those who had been waiting for promotions, or in some cases, he said, waiting for people to die. The new climate welcomed change. Many newsroom staffers had started at the bottom as copy boys and worked their way up to management. Some were classically educated, but few had degrees from journalism schools or had worked for other newspapers. Batten wanted to hire younger, better-educated visionaries who were more attuned to what was going on in the industry.

As part of the newspapers' metamorphosis, Batten hired the company's first personnel director, tapping L. Cameron "Cam" Gregory, the *Pilot*'s night assistant city editor. Little thought had gone into succession planning; jobs often were filled solely on an individual supervisor's instinct. Gregory brought seasoned professionals on board, many with MBAs or other advanced degrees. He instituted background checks on all new hires—references were contacted, previous employment was verified.

At Batten's urging, Gregory instituted management training and development. Executives were sent to seminars and workshops at Harvard and MIT, to Columbia University, and to the American Press Institute. An annual bonus plan for department heads was implemented, paid out of a pool based on the company's profitability. Gregory created a newsroom internship program to groom promising young reporters. Alliances were established with universities to identify the best and the brightest prospective employees.

Batten practiced "walk-around" management and learned employees' names. He looked back with pride at one of his first management decisions—the creation of a college tuition reimbursement program. Offering to pay for courses established the Norfolk newspapers as a progressive business determined to nurture its workforce. Old-timers in the newsroom poked fun at the new "college boys" Gregory had hired.

In his effort to transform a confederacy of "little chieftains" into a goal-oriented management team, Batten formed an operating committee and held group meetings with department heads. He won their respect by asking for their assessment of current conditions and what they thought ought to be done to make improvements. In 1957, Batten instituted the newspapers' first budgets.

According to John William "Bill" Diederich, another Harvard MBA who came to Norfolk in 1955 as the newspapers' first research director and became controller in 1961, departments didn't resist having to put together individual budgets because Batten never believed in squeezing them hard for money. Batten wanted his executives to look for ways to eliminate waste, improve productivity, and increase advertising rates, but he never went about it aggressively. "On the contrary," Diederich said, "we were pretty slow to raise rates over the years."[2]

With the advertising and accounting departments taking shape, Batten gradually ratcheted up the professionalism of the newsroom. That was no simple task. Edwin "Ed" Brandt was brought on board to help rebuild the news operation.

After Brandt talked Batten into a sports travel budget and a central copy desk, working conditions were next on his agenda. He told Batten and managing editor Robert H. Mason, "You can't have newsmen working in squalor."[3] Batten agreed, and equipment was upgraded. But reporters and editors always have taken a certain amount of pride in working in creative sordidness, so until filing cabinets and carpeted cubicles became permanent newsroom fixtures, until smoking was banned, and until near-noiseless word processors replaced manual typewriters, newsrooms continued to look like they had been ransacked.

Over time, Batten grew more confident in his decision making. One early area of concern was the afternoon *Ledger's* falling circulation. The *Virginian-Pilot* had been the weaker of the two newspapers until World War II when newsprint was rationed and the *Ledger's* news hole was cut back. The *Pilot* gained readership and surpassed the *Ledger* in circulation.

To stem the loss of afternoon readers, Batten urged his uncle to buy the *Portsmouth Star,* the competing evening newspaper. Batten surmised that acquiring circulation in Portsmouth would preserve the *Ledger.*

Slover, who had once co-owned the *Star,* agreed. In March 1955, only four and a half months after Batten had become publisher of Norfolk Newspapers, Slover repurchased the *Star.* He paid $1 million for the newspaper that he and his partners had sold thirty-one years earlier for $75,000.[4]

The transition was anything but smooth. The *Star*'s pressmen, its printers in particular, assumed Slover would shut down the paper. Many left their jobs for the *Ledger* and the *Pilot.* Before long, there barely were enough pressmen to get the *Star* on the street.

To make matters worse, the Portsmouth community felt betrayed. Many Portsmouth readers and advertisers regarded their city with a protective pride; the river separating them from bigger, better-known Norfolk might just as well have been as wide as the Atlantic. Within a year, a former *Star* advertising salesman convinced a group of Portsmouth merchants to invest in an independent new daily called the *Portsmouth Times,* competing head-to-head with the *Star.* Its first issue was published on May 6, 1956. Many *Star* employees moved to the new paper, including William T. "Bill" Leffler Jr. He was shocked when the *Star* was sold and accepted an offer as sports editor of the *Times* where salaries were double and triple what the *Ledger* was paying.[5]

Batten said years later that while he and Slover had no plans to combine the *Ledger* and *Star,* it would have happened eventually—and the competition from the fledgling competitor only sped the process. When the merger was announced in 1957, the company tried to soften the blow to make up for the psychological loss of the *Star.* Norfolk Newspapers Inc. was changed to Norfolk-Portsmouth Newspapers Inc. In Norfolk editions, the *Ledger-Dispatch* front-page flag flew above the *Portsmouth Star,* which was set in smaller type. In papers bound for Portsmouth newspaper subscribers, the *Portsmouth Star* flag dominated, the *Ledger-Dispatch* appearing in small type beneath it. Even though the *Ledger* was giving Portsmouth residents more local news as part of a $2 million expansion of the Norfolk newspapers' production facility, Portsmouth wanted its own newspaper.

The upstart *Portsmouth Times* took advantage of the situation, snatching local advertising. Batten organized weekly strategy sessions to fight back. "In the end, that competition turned out to be the best thing that happened to me and the organization," Batten said. "It welded the organization together. Ever since then, I've always thought that having a common enemy is the best thing to stimulate morale and a cooperative effort in any kind of organization, whether a company or a community."

An effort was made by Sheldon Sackett, an eccentric West Coast newspaperman, to salvage the *Times*. He set himself up in a big suite at a Norfolk hotel. "He was giving away money like it was paper," Batten said, noting that Sackett would order champagne with dinner and give the bellhop a $50 tip. "That was big money in those days. It was like he was sent from heaven to give away money all over town." Leffler, who would later remember Sackett as a "millionaire nut," quit the *Times* and returned to the *Ledger*.

The flamboyant Sackett blew out of town and the ten-month-old *Portsmouth Times* folded on March 24, 1957. It was not something Batten openly celebrated. But it was his first taste of victory, and he savored it.

Putting Down Roots

FAMILY AND COMMUNITY

ROM TIME TO TIME the Colonel had asked Batten why he wasn't married yet. He was the last bachelor among a group of friends who frequented the same Virginia Beach clubs, where they dined, danced, and gambled—although in August 1955, the *Virginian-Pilot* did an exposé on gambling at the Piney Point, Surf, and Dunes clubs, including photos of prominent citizens taken with Batten's own Minox spy camera.

As publisher, he wanted his newspapers to do the story—not because he had any moral feelings about gambling, which was illegal, but because it was a good story. *Virginian-Pilot* managing editor R. K. T. "Kit" Larson and Tom Hanes, managing editor of the evening *Ledger-Dispatch* flipped a coin to see which newspaper would do the story. Larson won. The article led to a special grand jury and eventually the end of gambling at the clubs. Batten, too, would move toward settling down in the summer of 1956.

That summer, after her freshman year at Hollins College in Roanoke, Jane Neal Parke worked in the newsroom of the *Virginian-Pilot*, first as secretary to the managing editor, and later in the photo department. Jane had been a frequent visitor to the Norfolk newspapers since she was a little girl, going to the office with her aunt, Mary Eugenia Parke, the *Pilot*'s first book page editor. Jane was the only child of a well-to-do family in Norfolk, and her parents had divorced. Her stepfather, Hunter Hogan, was chairman of a major Norfolk real estate firm and a feisty, outspoken civic leader.

Jane ran into Frank on the elevator a couple of times that summer. She was nineteen years old, he twenty-nine. Jane found him good looking, well-read, and interesting "in a strange sort of way."[1]

Robert N. Fishburn, who years later with his sister, Sally, sold the

Roanoke Times & World-News newspapers to Batten, knew him as a playboy who "cut a pretty broad path" across the state.[2] Batten confessed that he was being "ridiculously picky" by always looking for the perfect girl. "I would date a girl I thought was great and then I'd find something wrong with her." Batten was drawn to Jane by her intelligence and her aloofness. "She had sort of a quality that didn't make you feel like you could get real close to her and that attracted me," he said. "I don't really know why. . . . Whether it was 'I've got to break through this,' or what it was. And I always liked challenges."[3]

Jane is more matter-of-fact. "His family wanted him to get married. He figured it was time to get married and I just happened to appear." In September he asked her to be his wife. The wedding took place at Sacred Heart Catholic Church in Norfolk on February 23, 1957, with a reception for more than 200 guests at the Norfolk Yacht and Country Club. Batten had just turned thirty. Jane, nineteen, would celebrate her twentieth birthday on St. Patrick's Day.

The newlyweds spent their wedding night in New York and the next day flew to Montego Bay, Jamaica, for a week. They then headed for the snow-covered mountains of Stowe, Vermont, home of the von Trapp family from the *Sound of Music*. But Batten was an avid skier; his bride was a novice, so they couldn't go down the runs together. It turned her off to the sport, he said, and started the couple off on the wrong foot. Their ten-year age difference quickly became apparent. In hindsight, he would realize that it was the biggest problem they had to overcome. Until they were married, Jane lived at home and had a midnight curfew, which "wasn't all that unusual in those days," she said. Most of her friends tied the knot right out of college and maybe taught school until the babies came.

"Jane got married too young," Batten said. "I mean, she didn't have time to sow her oats like I did. And the fact that I was in this big job put pressure on her." Jane Batten was less delicate in her choice of words. "It has not been an easy marriage," she said. "I was too young and neither of us had an idea of what we were getting into."

Shortly after the birth of their first child, Frank Batten Jr.,[4] in July 1958, the family bought its first house in Norfolk's upscale Lochhaven section. Two daughters followed: Mary Elizabeth "Betsy" Batten, who would later take the name Maitri Leela Bavana, born in November 1960, and Dorothy Neal Batten, in December 1962.

Batten had been publisher for nearly three years when his eighty-four-year-old uncle all but stopped coming to the newspapers. The Colonel gave his nephew near total responsibility for the company, along with some advice: Set goals to produce good business results, and get involved in activities to benefit the community.

Batten understood the two tasks were inseparable. He knew that the newspapers' success depended on the growth of the South Hampton Roads region, which at the time was called Tidewater and included Norfolk, Portsmouth, the tiny hamlet of Virginia Beach, three mostly agricultural counties—Nansemond, Norfolk, and Princess Anne—and the peanut-processing town of Suffolk. The area had enormous potential.

In those early years, he was treasurer of the Norfolk Chamber of Commerce and twice served as general chairman of its International Azalea Court, created in 1953 to honor NATO, after the alliance's Atlantic Command moved to Norfolk. Among the most important community efforts Batten undertook was the week-long International Naval Review in June 1957. In what was to be billed as one of the largest peacetime assemblies of warships in history, one hundred ships from eighteen nations would line the harbor in pairs, the procession stretching for fourteen miles.[5]

The first Naval Review, commemorating the 300th anniversary of the Jamestown settlement, had taken place in Norfolk a half-century earlier, with President Theodore Roosevelt and Mark Twain among its guests.[6] The pressure on Batten to make the second review a success was intense. One of his biggest problems was trying to figure out what to do with the thousands of sailors descending on Hampton Roads. Batten met with U.S. Representative Porter Hardy Jr., Secretary of the Navy Thomas S. Gates Jr., and Chief of Naval Operations Admiral Arleigh A. Burke in Washington. "What are you going to do with all those foreign sailors?" they asked. "How are you going to entertain them?"

World War II Norfolk was still fresh in sailors' memories, and the city was struggling to overcome its wartime reputation as the country's roughest port. As the nation had readied for war, the federal government had added a thousand acres to the Norfolk Naval Base, and the city's population had ballooned from 144,000 to 368,000 inside of four years. Sailors and civilian employees hungry for work streamed into Norfolk and neighboring cities. The nearby Norfolk Navy Yard, which built forty-two warships and patched up or overhauled ships damaged during the war, had about 6,500 workers in 1940; within three years, 43,000.

City services—water and housing supply, schools, transportation —were overburdened. In the packed city streets, more than four hundred prostitutes peddled their wares in what *American Mercury* magazine in 1940 called "Our Worst War Town."[7] When the red light district was shut down by the city the following year, prostitutes moved to other parts of town or worked as "cab-girls," selling their services from many of the city's three hundred taxis. Urban legend has it that more than one "Dogs and sailors keep off the grass" sign was posted in neighborhoods. A federal housing administrator in the 1950s called the city's slums the "worst in the nation."[8]

Batten and local promoter Ben Wahrman convinced Harry Price, an appliance store owner and civic leader, to head up a campaign to get local businesses to buy tickets to give to the sailors for shows by the Ice Capades and the Ringling Brothers Circus. They also had to persuade each local city government to put up money to promote the event. Batten, Wahrman, and banker Sam Northern went to Princess Anne County's Board of Supervisors to ask for money to help support the event. It was before the county merged with Virginia Beach, and the area was largely rural; most board members were farmers.

Batten did the talking. The response was dead silence. "They sat there; didn't ask any questions," Batten said. "I've never had such a cold reception in my life. This group of farmers looked at us with cold, fishy eyes: 'Who are these city boys coming to rob us?'"

Bob Wahab, the city attorney for Princess Anne County, came to their rescue. "These are honest men," he told the supervisors. "I've known Mr. Batten and Mr. Northern for a long time. They are good people; they are honest people. They have made an honest presentation to you." To Batten's relief, the supervisors agreed to kick in money.

When Batten signed contracts with the circus, the Ice Capades, and the Norfolk Symphony in order to get on their schedules, he wasn't sure the money could be raised to pay them. He secured a line of credit for upwards of $1 million only by offering a personal guarantee.

"I had never guaranteed anything at that point," Batten said. "It was a huge amount of money for me." His friend and advisor Charles Kaufman cosigned. Eventually the region's cities came through with the money, and contributions from business leaders paid for tickets for 50,000 sailors to attend shows with such top-name performers as José Greco, Woody Herman, Gene Krupa, Carmen McRae, and Lionel Hampton.

On June 11, a sunny day with temperatures in the eighties, the ships began steaming out of their berths for the following day's full-dress parade in a show of Western might. With pennants flying, warships from the United States, Belgium, Canada, Colombia, Cuba, Denmark, the Dominican Republic, France, Great Britain, Italy, the Netherlands, Norway, Peru, Portugal, Spain, Turkey, Uruguay, and Venezuela lined the harbor. Rear Admiral Claude V. Ricketts, commander of Destroyer Flotilla Four, choreographed their movements from a blimp. A flotilla of private boats passed in review.

A special 100-page souvenir edition of the *Norfolk Ledger-Dispatch* and the *Portsmouth Star* touted the event. Admiral Jerauld Wright, NATO's supreme allied commander, authored the lead story, in which he noted that his command was ready "with a formidable force that stands as a primary deterrent to Soviet aggression."

The Naval Review was a success. It drew national and international attention to Norfolk. Batten was worn out after working nonstop. He'd been overwhelmed with duties at the newspaper, other community activities, and his new marriage, besides. Never before had he been responsible to so many for so much.

Exhausted, he fell ill "with one of those damn viruses" that he couldn't shake for three months. But his success firmly established Batten's role as a community leader.

8 Taking a Stand

I N 1951, THE National Association for the Advancement of Colored People, on behalf of 117 African American high school students in Farmville—a rural Virginia town near Appomattox, where Gen. Robert E. Lee surrendered to end the Civil War—filed a federal lawsuit asking for facilities on a par with schools for whites. The court ruled that equal facilities had to be provided for the black students, but refused to allow them to attend a white school before a new school was built. The NAACP's appeal to the U.S. Supreme Court became part of the *Brown v. Board of Education of Topeka (Kansas)* case, along with NAACP-sponsored lawsuits from Delaware, South Carolina, and the District of Columbia.

In 1954, the U.S. Supreme Court ruled that "separate educational facilities are inherently unequal." The decision prompted the greatest social change in the South since Reconstruction, setting in motion a wave of federal laws that would eventually protect the rights of people of color and women, including the Equal Pay Act of 1963, the Civil Rights Act of 1964, and the Voting Rights Act of 1965.

Virginian-Pilot editorial page editor Joseph Lenoir Chambers Jr. vigorously backed the Supreme Court decision. Joseph A. Leslie Jr., editorial page editor of the *Ledger-Dispatch,* its evening sister newspaper, took the opposing position, calling for continued separation of black and white students. It was a policy unique in southern journalism for papers owned by the same company and in the same town to take contradictory positions on the same issue.[1] But Samuel Slover firmly believed in a hands-off policy with his editorial page editors, even if he personally opposed their opinions.

While editorial policy traditionally reflects the viewpoint of a newspaper's publisher and owner, Slover's philosophy had been based in part on the strength of his editorial writers. In 1929, Louis Jaffe Sr. had won a Pulitzer Prize, journalism's most prestigious award, for his *Virginian-Pilot* editorials denouncing the Ku Klux Klan, condemning racist laws, and almost single-handedly persuading then-Governor Harry F. Byrd to introduce the strongest anti-lynching legislation in the South.

Batten, who was named publisher of the Norfolk newspapers five months after the *Brown v. Board of Education* ruling, likewise did not interfere with the newspapers' editorials. It was a decision that eventually would haunt him, and one that he would reluctantly and painfully reverse.

Within two hours of the landmark Supreme Court ruling, Virginia Governor Thomas Stanley called for "cool heads, calm, steady and sound judgment."[2] J. Lindsay Almond Jr., his attorney general, urged the state to be rational. But when Byrd, now a U.S. senator and a committed segregationist, heard their reactions, "the top blew off the U.S. Capitol,"[3] according to Almond.

Because of the strong influence of both the Navy and NATO, Norfolk was seen as a liberal southern city unlike Richmond and Petersburg, its parochial, more insular neighbors. Norfolk's citizens appeared to take the Supreme Court decision calmly. The school superintendent allowed that while he was not in favor of integration, he wanted to carry out the court's decree "with the least harm to pupils."

A week after the ruling, Governor Stanley invited five black leaders, including the publisher of the minority-owned *Norfolk Journal and Guide,* to the state capitol in Richmond and urged them to voluntarily accept segregation. They refused. The following month, he met with twenty state legislators at a fire station in predominantly black Petersburg, and in another meeting rallied governors or their representatives from a dozen southern states to resist integrating schools. Stanley vowed to "use every legal means" to keep Virginia's schools segregated.

That August, the governor appointed a thirty-two member all-white legislative commission—there were no black legislators—to study the implications of the Supreme Court ruling. State Senator Garland Gray, who chaired the commission, issued a preliminary report in January 1955. Its conclusion: Forced integration would destroy the Virginia public school system.

The initial U.S. Supreme Court ruling had not mandated how integration would take place, but in May 1955 the *Brown II* ruling decreed that public schools should be integrated "with all deliberate speed." That autumn, Virginia attorney general Almond, who had initially called for temperance, now said that the only way to deal with the issue was to "Seg 'em . . . and keep shoving segregation down their throats until the good people rise up and make you do the right thing."[4]

The legislative commission issued its final report, known as the Gray Plan, the following month. To minimize the number of black students entering white schools, local school boards would assign pupils to schools. The report also called for a statewide referendum to amend the state constitution. If approved by voters, taxpayer dollars would be used to pay for private schools for parents who chose not to send their children to integrated public schools. If voters rejected the idea, the governor admonished, they would be voting for "mixed schools in Virginia."[5]

Batten's *Ledger-Dispatch* enthusiastically endorsed passage of the referendum. Its morning sister balked, countering that it flew in the face of the state's doctrine that public money should not be used to pay for private education and would result in a dismantling of the public school system. Every major state newspaper and many of Virginia's leaders endorsed the change in state law, leaving the *Virginian-Pilot* nearly alone in the debate.

On a cold, rainy Monday in January 1956, Virginia voters endorsed the measure by more than a two-to-one margin. Further cementing its position, a month later the Virginia General Assembly adopted an "Interposition Resolution," invoking state sovereignty as a way to keep the federal government's nose out of the state's business. *Richmond News Leader* editor James J. Kilpatrick had pushed the doctrine's virtues in a two-month editorial campaign.[6] In Norfolk, the *Ledger* saw it largely as a symbolic protest. The *Pilot* called it an "exercise in fantasy."[7]

Byrd was not appeased by either strategy, and his opinion mattered. For a half-century Byrd had led a powerful Democratic political fiefdom known as the Byrd Organization. Seen by some as Virginia's most powerful political leader in the twentieth century, his organization was unrivaled nationally for its three-decade control of state politics. His was one of Virginia's oldest families—among his ancestors were said to be Pocahontas and the founder of the city of Richmond. He was Virginia's governor from 1926 to 1930 and U.S. senator from 1933 to 1965. Almond claimed that nothing of substance happened, or was supposed to happen, in Virginia's political realm without the former governor's assent.

As far as Byrd was concerned, not nearly enough was being done to circumvent the Supreme Court's decree. He rallied the like-minded and in February 1956 called for a program of "massive resistance" to desegregation. He sanctimoniously demanded that Virginia take the lead in maintaining separate schools in the South. Standing on a flatbed truck behind stacked cans of applesauce at an annual picnic in his Winchester orchards, Byrd thundered: "If Virginia surrenders, if Virginia's line is broken, the rest of the South will go down, too."[8]

In March, Byrd and Senator Strom Thurmond of South Carolina crafted the "Southern Manifesto," calling the Supreme Court decision an abuse of power and pledging to use all lawful means to reverse it. It was signed by 101 congressmen, including Virginia's dozen U.S. representatives and senators.

The Norfolk chapter of the NAACP filed its first school desegregation lawsuit in Norfolk's federal court in May 1956. The suit landed on the desk of Judge Walter E. "Beef" Hoffman, who earned his nickname in his scrappy youth in South Orange, New Jersey. A Republican who had been appointed to the U.S. District Court's Eastern District of Virginia by President Eisenhower two years earlier, Hoffman, forty-nine, was known for his no-nonsense approach to litigation and rapidly earned a reputation as a distinguished and independent jurist. No friend to the Byrd Organization, Hoffman had shattered the color barriers in Norfolk's public transportation system a month earlier and would do the same with its city parks. Determined to enforce the Supreme Court's ruling, Hoffman was shunned by all but a few close friends. Undaunted, he said he would do his duty "if it costs me my last friend on earth."[9]

In September 1956, both the Virginia House and Senate deployed another weapon from its segregationist armory, the Stanley Plan, named after the governor. Instead of local school boards assigning students to schools, a three-member Pupil Placement Board appointed by the governor now would take over the job. There was a catch. If a white school admitted a black student, either voluntarily or by court order, the state would close the school. Even if city lawmakers petitioned the governor to reopen an integrated school, the state would stop writing checks to the local school system.

The Norfolk School Board had taken a moderate stand on the order to integrate. While pressured by local and state politicos to hold out, the board correctly anticipated that the federal courts eventually would force schools to be opened to blacks. The board members believed it was more important to keep Norfolk public schools open than to conform to state policies.

The *Ledger* supported the Stanley Plan, acknowledging that some schools likely would be shut down. "There is no question that Virginians as a whole wish to maintain a solid wall of resistance against classroom integration," Leslie wrote. "A fundamental purpose would be to deter Negro children from applying for admission to white schools in the first place."[10] The *Pilot* expressed astonishment. School closures were "an appalling reality," judged *Pilot* editor Chambers. "Once the standards are gone, the work of a generation may be destroyed."[11]

In June 1958, Judge Hoffman ordered the Norfolk School Board to assign 151 black applicants to previously all-white schools for the following school year; other federal judges ordered Arlington, Charlottesville, and Warren County to do likewise. Those orders ran headlong into state laws passed two years earlier requiring any public school that ended its whites-only policy to shut down. If schools closed, the state reasoned, calm would prevail and federal troops would not be required to integrate a public school as had happened in Little Rock, Arkansas, at the beginning of the previous school year.

Wrote the *Pilot*'s Chambers on June 20: "If our schools are closed, not only our children suffer, but the entire city will be severely damaged economically. Norfolk's black eye on the national scene as a result of closed schools would be one of the most disastrous effects." Crippled, he declared, would be "every aspect of the economic wellbeing of our city."

The Norfolk School Board was caught in the middle. Judge Hoffman's federal ruling required the city with "reasonable promptness and without regard to race" to evaluate black students' requests to attend white schools; the State Supreme Court of Appeals issued an injunction on August 18 prohibiting the board from enrolling students in any school. The same day, the School Board rejected all 151 blacks.

Three days later, Judge Hoffman met with School Board members, reiterated the U.S. Supreme Court's mandate and said the threat of school closures by the state was not enough reason for refusing to approve the transfers. At the end of August, the School Board reluctantly agreed to admit seventeen black students to six of Norfolk's white junior and senior high schools. The *Pilot* and the *Ledger* continued their editorial tug of war.

"There is no moral justification for the harsh punishment of the state's largest city by locking up its junior and senior high schools because its School Board, pursuant to law and the direction of a court, will assign a handful of Negro pupils to schools where other pupils are white," the *Virginian-Pilot*'s Chambers wrote on August 30. "Surely there is greater wisdom in Virginia than this would imply." The *Ledger-Dispatch*, on the other hand, blamed forced integration on "the federal machinery and those who have set the court machinery in motion."

On September 8, 1958, Almond, who had been elected Virginia's governor earlier that year, ordered Warren County schools in the Shenandoah Valley closed. Two weeks later, Almond's picture was on the cover of *Time* magazine. The governor, who had vowed that he would give his right arm before a black was admitted to a white school, next closed two schools in Charlottesville, the home of the University of Virginia. On September 27, he ordered six Norfolk schools to close, barring nearly 10,000 children from schools that would remain chained and padlocked for the next five months. He assumed complete jurisdiction over the closed schools. Almost overlooked in the resulting tumult were the rest of Norfolk's elementary schools, three black secondary schools, and one white junior high, none of which had been ordered to integrate. Each opened for classes as usual.

The *Pilot*'s Chambers proclaimed the closures "unjust and cruel" and called the imbroglio "an injustice against which Norfolk people are already showing that they will protest in the full conviction that the state has no moral right—and probably no legal right—to punish them thus."[12]

Mayor W. Fred Duckworth called for a referendum to let voters decide if schools should be returned to city control, reopened, and integrated. The referendum ballots added a caveat: If the schools reopened parents would have to pay "a substantial tuition"[13] for each child to make up for severed state funding. The November 18 initiative, which voters rejected by a three-to-two margin, was seen as a fraud by the *Pilot*'s Chambers. The *Ledger*'s Leslie said voters had shown that "they'd resist school integration even at the cost of closed schools."

Later described as "the epitome of the urban political boss with his stocky, even pudgy, five-foot, ten-and-a-half-inch frame, and jowly visage,"[14] Duckworth's star was rising in the Byrd Organization, and it was he, not Almond, who was seen as the hero of massive resistance. Education wasn't all that suffered. As Chambers had predicted, economic development slowed to a crawl in Norfolk; both the military and civilian businesses were unwilling to invest or expand in a state that refused to educate its children. Some companies already had decided not to locate in Virginia until the school issue was resolved. Virginia as a whole suffered.

As the vice president of the local Chamber of Commerce, Batten knew that the business community was divided on the issue. That fall, Batten had told chamber president Pretlow Darden, who also was a former city councilman, that he was concerned about the effects of closure on the local economy. Darden had agreed massive resistance was a mistake, but told Batten that it would be better to hold off taking a public stance until the Virginia Supreme Court made a decision on the matter.

In the meantime, Norfolk and Western Railroad chairman Stuart Saunders formed the Virginia Industrialization Group, an association of influential business leaders aimed at bolstering the crippled economy. Batten was the only newspaper publisher in Virginia to sign on. The group's spokesmen were Batten and Lewis Powell, a corporate attorney and the head of the Richmond School Board, who in 1972 was appointed by President Richard Nixon to the U.S. Supreme Court, where he served for twenty-five years.[15]

"We all said, 'Look, we can't be very successful in developing the economy and getting industry to come here as long as we've got massive resistance and our schools are closed,'"[16] Batten recalled. "What is it we as a group can do to try to moderate this radical position of the state and get rid of massive resistance?" In December, Batten and twenty-eight other business leaders met with Governor Almond, the lieutenant governor, and the attorney general in a private, unpublicized dinner at the elite Rotunda Club in Richmond's 1895 Jefferson Hotel.

After dinner, Batten and several others stood and told the governor that Virginia's economy was going to be damaged in a "very severe way" because of its massive resistance policies. "Virginia ought to come to its senses and reopen the schools and get on with education," Batten recalled telling Almond.

The governor responded with a ten-minute harangue, angrily shaking his finger. He was incensed over the editorial position of the *Pilot*. He resented what he called unfair editorials about the state policy and about him personally. None of the editorials had taken personal shots at him, in matter of fact, but they obviously had criticized his actions as governor. "He said we'd live to rue the day we'd written them," Batten recalled.

On January 13, 1959, the Norfolk City Council, at Duckworth's urging, voted six-to-one to stop funding all the city's schools beyond the sixth grade. Affected were an additional 1,914 white students and 5,259 black pupils. Councilman Roy B. Martin Jr., a Duckworth appointee, was the only one who stood up to Duckworth. Looking back on his vote many years later, Martin said it would have been "stupid" to worsen the problem by closing more schools.[17] Bolstered by Martin's vote and alarmed by Duckworth's extremism, the School Board issued a statement indicating its displeasure with the latest round of school closings.

The *Virginian-Pilot* continued to be seen as an emotional anchor and an advocate of restraint and good judgment. Chambers called the action by City Council the "cruelest blow of all" to the city's schools. "It was not that the editorials were read by a wide audience throughout the state," Batten pointed out, "but they were read avidly by politicians."

If the *Pilot*'s editorials were beacons, the *Ledger-Dispatch*'s editorials were shipwrecks. Batten agonized over his hands-off policy allowing editorials that lauded the virtues of massive resistance. He no longer read Leslie's expatiations. Finally, after many sleepless nights, Batten resolved to reverse the evening paper's editorial position.

Looking back decades later, Batten tried to explain his rationale. "When the publisher realizes that the editorial policy is not only wrong but damaging to the community . . ." He paused. "I had rationalized for a long time that we were providing a balanced viewpoint, that we should let the people make up their own minds. But then it came to a point where I decided the *Ledger*'s editorials were giving too much comfort to the segregationists and to massive resistance." The editorial page's position was damaging to the community and in the end would be damaging to the paper, he said. "I wish I had changed the *Ledger* a lot sooner."

On January 19, Robert E. Lee's birthday and a legal state holiday, the Virginia Supreme Court of Appeals declared that closing schools violated the state constitution's guarantee of free public education. In a ruling timed to coincide with the state's decision, a three-judge federal court panel sitting in Norfolk determined the school closing laws illegal under the U.S. Constitution as well. The decision was written by Judge Hoffman. "Together the two decisions not only knock down . . . they also clear away the rubbish," wrote Chambers. "For the rest, a historic opportunity now opens for Virginians. The great of heart and mind will rise to it."

Batten sat down with Leslie and told him to write an editorial reversing the *Ledger*'s long-standing views supporting segregated schools. Leslie asked Batten to write it. The shift in policy was so gradual that Batten and others have no concrete recollection of which editorial he wrote changing the *Ledger*'s views on massive resistance. Batten believes it was published on January 20, 1959.

Under the headline "Massive Resistance Breaks Down," the editorial stated that it was "apparent that school closing as a weapon against integration had been outlawed. And the *Ledger-Star,* which had fought for school segregation with every persuasive means at its command, reluctantly concludes that massive resistance as we have known it has come to an end, and it becomes necessary now for those who believe in segregation to seek some other field from which to carry on the fight."

The Supreme Court "made a tragic mistake when it decreed the abolition of segregation in public schools . . . and it will haunt the United States for many years to come," the editorial continued. It had been "necessary to provide a voice in this area to speak for the vast majority of Tidewater citizens, who are opposed to integration. This newspaper has undertaken to provide that voice."

The editorial then reiterated the paper's newfound opposition to segregation, concluding that "it is just as clear that closing the schools, or abandoning any considerable segment of the public school system, will not be the final answer." And that "with massive resistance in collapse, it is quite evident that those who have relied upon it as a solution of the integration problem will have to accept something less."

Batten grimaced at the recollection of the editorial. "I have to say I'm embarrassed because it was a terrible editorial," he said. "It reads like the writer was tortured, but I was tortured. I was writing with my hands tied behind my back. We were reversing our position and there wasn't any good way to write that. How do you explain why all these years we've been strongly taking one position and now we're reversing it? How do you do that without it sounding dumb? I didn't want to put any more egg on Joe Leslie's face than I had to. It was a bad editorial, but it accomplished the purpose."

Two days later, President Eisenhower voiced his concern about the absence of education for children of federal workers in Norfolk, and hinted that his patience was wearing thin. That evening, CBS aired "The Lost Class of '59," an hour-long documentary by journalists Edward R. Murrow and Fred W. Friendly spotlighting the closed Norfolk schools. Many local residents, some of whom had taken no position during the wearying ordeal, were appalled to see how the rest of the country viewed their city.

Darden telephoned Batten at his Brambleton Avenue office. "Frank," he said. "It's time." Instead of getting the Chamber of Commerce directly involved, Batten and Darden solicited former mayors, chamber officers, the Hampton Roads Maritime Association, the Norfolk Port Authority, and many of the city's business and professional leaders.

On January 26, the long-silent business community spoke. In a full-page *Virginian-Pilot* ad, one hundred of Norfolk's leading business, professional, and civic leaders petitioned the City Council to reopen the schools. Batten and Darden coauthored the ad, and each paid half its cost. Charles Kaufman, Batten's legal advisor and confidant, helped with compromise wording that would be acceptable to those whose signatures they sought. They settled on capping the list at a hundred signatures. "Otherwise," Batten said, "where do you cut it off?"

The petition read:

> While we would strongly prefer to have segregated schools, it is evident from the recent court decisions that our public schools must either be integrated to the extent legally required or must be abandoned. The abandonment of our public school system is, in our opinion, unthinkable, as it would mean the denial of an adequate education to a majority of our children. Moreover, the consequences would be most damaging to our community. We, therefore, urge the Norfolk City Council to do everything within its power to open all public schools as promptly as possible.

Batten faced a formidable challenge. The business community had resisted challenging Byrd because it favored the senator's stand on low taxes and antiunion legislation. Batten not only risked alienating his peers, but by using his newspapers as the forum for the petition to the City Council, he knew *Pilot* and *Ledger* subscriptions could be canceled en masse. By taking such a visible stance, he also risked putting himself and his family—which now included his first child, Frank Jr.—in physical danger. A University of North Carolina study conducted after the court decisions, but before the schools reopened, found that 80 percent of Norfolk's white residents continued to support segregated schools.[18]

Batten and Darden collected most of the signatures in one day. Mayor Duckworth was furious when he caught wind of what was going on. He telephoned the pair, "raised hell and told us we ought not to publish it," Batten said. "He was very angry and told us we were doing terrible damage to the city.

"'We're sorry you feel that way,' we said, and kept collecting signatures."

Duckworth immediately began contacting some of the signers, who came to be known as the Committee of 100. The mayor insisted they take their names off the petition. Batten said only one person had second thoughts. Batten told the man they'd strike his name from the petition if he wanted them to. He said he'd call back. He never did, so his name was left on.

The following day, real estate executive Harvey Lindsay pulled together thirty-five of the city's younger business and civic leaders, who presented their own petition to the City Council. The *Virginian-Pilot* hailed the business community as a "new clear voice" and welcomed its "striking and welcome change."[19]

The Committee of 100's advertisement was published in the *Pilot* only five days before schools reopened. Batten later said the petition drive would have failed had it been attempted earlier. Nor did he particularly like the wording of the petition, which was hardly an endorsement of equality.

"You have to understand the climate of the time," Batten said. "It's not easy to explain to someone who didn't live through it. The vast majority of white people were raised from the time they were tiny children to believe blacks and whites should be segregated. They accepted it as the way the world works." The petition was, quite simply, a "graceful retreat before the onslaught of economic law," according to an observer in 1960. The bottom line: Closing schools was bad for business.

A defeated Governor Almond abruptly reversed course and without explanation advised the legislature to accept the courts' decisions. On February 2, with President Eisenhower receiving hourly reports via a special telephone hookup to the Norfolk federal courthouse, the doors of the city's six white secondary schools were opened 141 days after they'd been padlocked. With the international press descending on Norfolk to cover the story, Batten directed reporters from both of his newspapers to keep a low profile—to do nothing to keep the schools from reopening peacefully.

On a blustery winter morning, with temperatures hovering in the mid-twenties, seventeen blacks joined white students at six secondary schools without major incident. Lenoir Chambers's *Pilot* editorial applauded Virginians for a "display of sanity and poise and dignity that made a difficult day a notable day."

"The public schools are back in business," he wrote. "That is the flame of achievement that rises highest in the day's events. Every man and woman in Virginia ought to resolve anew to keep that flame burning."

While schools were now legally mandated to integrate, the five-year battle nevertheless continued to fester. All but ignored by the bureaucrats were the fate and feelings of students, pawns in a lengthy political, legislative, and court battle. Some 2,700 of the city's nearly 10,000 students never returned to complete their educations. Many had moved away; others quit school and got jobs; still others married or joined the military.

Batten and Darden's petition, more than anything, turned the tide of public opinion in Norfolk, according to Harvey Lindsay, because it represented a melding of the old guard, led by Pretlow Darden, and the new guard, "which was Frank."[20] Given that most readers of Batten's newspapers wanted segregated schools, Batten could have followed the lead of other publishers around the state and the South. Instead, he followed his conscience and chose to back Chambers. Bob Mason, the *Pilot*'s associate editor under Chambers and later its editor, believed, however, that if Batten had been more experienced, he might have unified the newspapers' editorial positions from the start.

"If he had been thirty-five at the outset (he was twenty-seven), I think he would have gone to them and said, 'Look, it's too bad you feel differently, but we aren't going to give the appearance of working both sides of the street. We've got to agree on a course on this thing, and there's going to be unity.'"[21] Chambers's biographer likewise concluded that had Batten acted sooner, Leslie would have had to reverse or drastically modify his stand or relinquish his editorship. Consistency in the message from the region's two leading newspapers then would have "magnified its effect manifold."[22]

Chambers's unwavering message to *Pilot* readers that Norfolk should peacefully carry out the Supreme Court's ruling to desegregate its public schools earned him a Pulitzer Prize in 1960. The morning he learned he had won, he telephoned a downtown Norfolk typewriter store. "I've just won the Pulitzer Prize," he announced, "and I'm coming down there to buy a new typewriter." He used the rest of his $2,000 award to build a powder room for his wife.

After Batten reversed the *Ledger*'s editorial policy, it was agreed that Leslie would no longer write about massive resistance or school integration. For the rest of Leslie's life, the two men never discussed the topics again. Leslie retired as the *Ledger*'s editor on June 1, 1959, not because he was angry and not because he was forced out, Batten said, but because he had reached the newspaper's mandatory retirement age. The Norfolk City Council presented him with a Certificate of Outstanding Service.

Byrd remained in Congress and continued to fight for southern and states' rights, including opposing the Voting Rights Act of 1965. He died the following year of an inoperable brain tumor. Norfolk's Mayor Duckworth kept a framed copy of Batten's Committee of 100 petition tacked to the back of his office door so he'd be reminded of the men he considered traitors every time he closed his door. "He hated every one of them,"[23] remembered Batten's friend Jack Rixey, a former state legislator. In 1972, Duckworth was gunned down near his Norfolk home; his murder has never been solved.

Did Batten look back with satisfaction at the part he played in those dark days? "Pride would be accurate, but not satisfaction," he'd later say. "You can't look back at a time when a lot of kids were out of school with any satisfaction. The part I'm not proud of was that the *Ledger* took the wrong position. It did give a source of comfort to the segregationists."

Colonel Slover, who was "very much opposed to massive resistance," according to Batten, died on November 29, 1959, less than a year after schools reopened and two years after leaving his beloved newspaper office for the last time. He was eighty-six.

Batten was eating breakfast when he got the phone call. Even though he had known that the Colonel was near death, the news was devastating. "All of a sudden I broke out crying," he said. It was the only time as an adult that he had shed tears.

Frank Batten's mother, Dorothy Martin Batten, as a girl. She died in 1964, at the age of 61. (Courtesy of the Batten family)

Frank Batten, who died of pneumonia at the age of 31 in 1928, when his son, Frank, was a year old. (Courtesy of the Batten family)

(*Above*) Frank Batten and his uncle, "Colonel" Samuel Slover. Frank and his mother moved in with the Slovers in their Norfolk, Virginia, home after Frank's father died. (Courtesy of the Batten family)

(*Right*) Frank dressed up as Blackbeard, 1931. (Courtesy of the Batten family)

(*Left*) Frank Batten at the age of 7. He grew up in Norfolk with his mother, aunt, and uncle. (Courtesy of the Batten family)

(*Below*) Frank christens his aunt's yacht, the *Shadow Fay,* in 1934. (Courtesy of the Batten family)

Frank Batten graduated from Culver Military Academy in 1945 and entered the U.S. Merchant Marine Academy. (Courtesy of the Batten family)

Jane and Frank Batten were married in Norfolk, Virginia, on February 23, 1957. (Courtesy of the Batten family)

(*Right*) Jane and Frank Batten in 1963. (Courtesy of the Batten family)

(*Below*) Frank Jr., Betsy (Leela), and Dorothy Batten. (Courtesy of the Batten family)

Frank Batten and crew on *Shadow* at the end of the Newport Bermuda race in 1976. *Shadow* was one of several racing boats he owned that were named after his Aunt Fay Slover's yacht, the *Shadow Fay*. (Courtesy of the Batten family)

The Batten family owned a home in Aspen. On the slopes, from left, are Betsy (Leela), Frank, Jane, Frank Jr., and Dorothy Batten. (Courtesy of the Batten family)

Frank Batten Jr., Frank IV, James, and Aimee Batten. (Courtesy of the Batten family)

Admiral Jerauld Wright introduces Jane Batten to King Hussein of Jordan in 1958. (Courtesy of the Batten family)

John Coleman, whose idea it was to create the Weather Channel, at left, and Frank Batten, who took a chance on backing it financially when no one else would, at a July 1981 press conference in New York announcing the launch of the network. (Courtesy of the Batten family)

Frank Batten with President Ronald Reagan at the White House in 1984. At right is Keith Fuller, president of the Associated Press from 1976 to 1985. Batten was chairman of the AP from 1982 to 1987 and was a member of its board for twelve years. (Courtesy of the Batten family)

Japanese Emperor Hirohito meets Frank Batten and other AP board members in 1984. (Courtesy of the Batten family)

Nancy Reagan and Frank Batten at the annual meeting of the AP in May 1987. Reagan was the keynote speaker. (Courtesy of the Batten family)

Former British Prime Minister Margaret Thatcher was chancellor of the College of William and Mary in Williamsburg, Virginia, from 1993 to 2000. She awarded Batten, a member of the college's board, an honorary doctorate in 1996. (Courtesy of the Batten family)

Frank Batten strongly believed that newspapers have the ability to tell stories in depth in a way in which other contemporary media are unable to do. (Courtesy of Denis Finley, the *Virginian-Pilot*)

9 Branching Out

THE BEGINNING OF LANDMARK

I N 1961, BATTEN MADE his first overtures to the Greensboro News Company, today, the *Greensboro News & Record*. Although he had passed up an opportunity to buy the Charlotte, North Carolina, *Observer*, because of concerns that his management team wasn't ready,[1] he had decided to diversify. He could not rely on the Norfolk papers alone to be the company's long-term economic engine and began to focus on acquiring businesses that had strong community ties and quality management.

Greensboro has a rich history and a friendly, small-town feel, belying its status as North Carolina's third-largest city. Named after Revolutionary War hero Nathanael Greene, it is a financial, insurance, and distribution hub and home to several universities and colleges. In 1960, four black students from North Carolina A&T sat down at a whites-only lunch counter at the F. W. Woolworth five-and-dime in downtown Greensboro and refused to leave until they'd been served. It was the first sit-in of the civil rights movement and set into motion similar protests throughout the South.

The newspapers had been controlled for fifty years by the family of Edwin Bedford "E.B." Jeffress. After a 1934 stroke, which had left him legally incompetent, Jeffress had held the courtesy title of president of the company. At his death in 1961, the newspapers—the *Greensboro Daily News* and its evening counterpart, the *Greensboro Record*—and the television station WFMY-TV had passed to Jeffress's five children, of whom only one, Charles O. "Carl" Jeffress, was working at the newspapers.

Nothing came of Batten's inquiry, or of overtures by other newspaper chains, including the *Washington Post*, until 1964. The Jeffress family were willing to sell but had three prerequisites for a new owner: Their tradition of public service had to be continued, along with a policy of promoting good government and the region's growth; the buyer must take a humanitarian outlook toward employees of the company; and there must be an understanding that the purchase entailed more than the mere transfer of stock ownership.[2]

Batten had benchmarks of his own that he insisted must be met with any acquisitions or start-ups: Would he get a better long-term return than with other opportunities? Were the risks tolerable? Did he understand the business, and have access to the talent to manage it successfully? Could he be proud of it?[3]

The deal appeared to meet the demands of both Batten and the Jeffress family. A price of $17,164,875 was agreed on. That was a heftier figure than Batten had expected, but he decided it was fair — and knew that the Greensboro News Company had several million dollars in the bank that became his with the purchase. The deal was sealed in a one-page agreement. "That was our contract: one page," Batten said.[4]

A few days later, media baron S. I. Newhouse Jr. and his younger brother, Donald, traveled to Greensboro with the thought of trumping Batten's bid. They liked what they saw and offered to top Batten's bid for the properties by $3 million to $4 million. But the Jeffress family stood by their agreement with Batten, whom Jeffress said best met the family's criteria in a new owner.

The transfer of ownership, in January 1965, was announced in a letter from Carl Jeffress in the *Daily News*.

> The new owners are men of integrity. They have a strong sense of corporate and community responsibility. They understand the dual nature of newspaper and television operations. They know that these properties are business ventures which must operate efficiently and produce a profit; but also know that they are, especially in the case of newspapers, institutions whose right to publish news and opinion with freedom is guaranteed by the Constitution.

ers in rural areas. Too far from broadcast towers to receive strong signals, they faced limited or poor reception that could be reduced to impenetrable in bad weather. In Roanoke Rapids, TV reception was so bad that most house roofs sported twenty-to-thirty-foot poles with antennas and rotors. If residents wanted to view a station out of Raleigh, the antenna was turned one way, another for Richmond, and still another for Norfolk. Even then the TV picture was snowy.

The cable business was fairly simple, with potentially excellent returns. Municipalities sought bids from cable companies and typically awarded a fifteen-year franchise to the system operator they deemed best for their communities. The cable operator built a "head end"—antennas to receive distant signals and modulate them onto coaxial cables—strung the cables on telephone or power poles, and connected the lines to homes. Batten was drawn to cable's uncomplicated technology, and he was convinced that marketing one type of subscription was not unlike marketing another. At about the same time that he bought the Roanoke Rapids franchise, Batten okayed $12,000, or one dollar per household, to buy the Beckley, West Virginia, franchise and $6,000 to buy one in Princeton, West Virginia. Building systems for each community drove the costs up; the initial investment in Roanoke Rapids was roughly $500,000.

Batten put together a small team in Norfolk and, marrying "television" with "cable," named the new business TeleCable. He hired Rex Bradley, whom he had met at Harvard Business School, to run it. Dick Roberts, who had worked in the *Virginian-Pilot*'s marketing research department, became vice president of operations. TeleCable was designed to be what its managers called a cost-containing "loose-tight" organization.[12] Programming, engineering, human resources, and marketing departments were centralized in Norfolk. Each local manager, however, was empowered to hire and fire and make other key decisions.

TeleCable was a business that required patience and a willingness to invest in the future. It produced large tax losses through the accelerated depreciation of its construction costs. The parent com-

The owners of Norfolk-Portsmouth Newspapers Inc. have a capacity for continuing dynamic growth and a willingness to accept new challenges. They also have a determination to carry out any mission to which they dedicate their heart, mind and hand. They have a healthy ambition, becoming modesty and a modern outlook. They are abreast of changes in the communications field and alert to capitalize on them. They are keenly interested in public affairs and recognize the important role of communication in the life of the 20th century. The best way to gauge their standards is to examine the excellent quality of their product in Norfolk.[5]

Batten published a statement the same day. He assured readers that the newspapers' executives would be autonomous and that they would live in Greensboro, although oversight of WFMY-TV would shift to Norfolk. He pledged that both the newspapers and the TV station would be dedicated to public service.

The Greensboro properties were Batten's first acquisition after his uncle's death, and the debt was substantial. Batten had convinced the Colonel to spend $1 million for the *Portsmouth Star* in 1955, but the Greensboro properties required $5 million from the company's savings and another more than $10 million in bank loans, including $600,000 in annual installments and, after ten years, a $4.6 million balloon payment.[6] Colleagues were surprised that Batten was willing to take on the Greensboro debt, but he was convinced he could turn the unprofitable company around.

With the Greensboro newspapers operating in the red, it was obvious to Batten that new management was sorely needed. Batten named himself president of the newspapers and the television station; Paul Huber was appointed a vice president. Peter B. Bush, advertising director for the Norfolk newspapers, moved to Greensboro as general manager. Dick Hendricks, who had been the controller for the newspapers in Norfolk, went as assistant general manager the following year. Carl Jeffress was kept on as publisher and a director while William Saunders, the sales promotion manager for Sears,

Roebuck and Co. in Norfolk, who'd started his career in the *Pilot*'s advertising department, became ad director.

When Kenneth W. Baldwin Jr. arrived in Greensboro as the new personnel chief, the newspapers had no such office. He created detailed files. He developed hiring standards that included reference checks. A battery of tests were administered throughout the company. In production, for example, workers were quizzed on their mechanical, comprehension, and general aptitude skills. That led in some cases to employees in journeymen jobs becoming supervisors.

Batten announced that Norfolk's pension plan was being implemented in Greensboro. Workers would be given credit for their years of employment as if they always had been part of the plan. The benefit represented a $12 million to $13 million liability. Still, employees were suspicious. Batten wasn't a Carolinian, and some of the newspapers' managers lamented that "some foreigner from Virginia" had bought the papers.

The newspapers' physical plant had been neglected. The three-story brick building was dark and dirty. The heat and air conditioning barely worked. Sheet metal patched weak sections of the wooden floors. The equipment was antiquated. In Batten's view, the newspapers also suffered from what he called "wall-to-wall" unions. He considered it an insult to have unions between him and his employees.

To modernize the "back shop"—where workers setting type, printing, assembling, and bundling newspapers used outmoded equipment that required slow, tedious labor—jobs had to be eliminated. The unions threatened to strike.

Production was transitioning from ages-old hot lead typesetting to a new technology—photographic, or "cold," type—and the department's several hundred workers resisted the change and their coveted union-won comforts. In case the unions staged a walkout, senior managers taught non-union workers to operate the presses. Preparations were made to hire permanent back shop replacements. Several executives were sent to out-of-state "scab school" where they were trained to produce the paper with skeleton staffing.

The union-management relationship was so tenuous at some newspapers in the 1960s and 1970s that armed guards were necessary to keep the peace. But the union bosses in Greensboro never made good on their threats to strike. They held informational pickets to let the public know they were unhappy, and there was occasional verbal harassment, but there was no violence. In the end, unions left the Greensboro news operation without a stoppage, and the modernizing continued.[7] There never has been a strike at any of Batten's more than 100 daily and community newspapers.

Batten's friend Kay Graham wasn't so lucky. A five-month walkout by *Washington Post* unions had traumatized her management team. As with Greensboro, the *Post* was intent on eliminating redundant staff and procedures it felt threatened the paper's fiscal health. Contracts with nine of the *Post*'s unions expired on October 1, 1975. At 4 a.m. that day, after disabling fire extinguishers, *Post* pressmen set fire to one of the newspaper's nine presses. They ripped out electrical wiring and operating parts, stripped gears, and slashed newsprint rolls on the nine presses' seventy-two printing units. The pressroom foreman was severely beaten. Joined by the other craft unions, the pressmen walked out. The Newspaper Guild, incensed by the damage, refused to honor the picket line and kept working.[8]

Batten and Stan Cook of the *Chicago Tribune* visited Graham periodically to offer advice about handling the showdown.[9] After dinner in her Georgetown home one evening, Batten said he would send five *Virginian-Pilot* production employees to help repair *Post* presses. R. G. "Bud" Dashiell, the *Pilot*'s mechanical superintendent, was asked to supervise the electrical repair work. Dashiell was airlifted by helicopter to the roof of the *Post* to avoid potential violence at the picket line and stayed three weeks to repair damage.[10]

In 1964, prior to the purchase of the Greensboro newspapers, Batten had already taken the first steps to expand his business into an entirely different medium. That year, Batten's Norfolk-Portsmouth Newspapers Inc. paid $15,000 for the television cable franchise in tiny Roanoke Rapids, North Carolina, eighty-five miles southwest of Norfolk.[11] Cable television was at that time a necessity for view-

pany wrote off the losses immediately against its newspaper and TV profits, and since the business was a private company, there was little concern about recording big book losses.

Publishers at Batten's newspapers were skeptical about the new business. "We were the skunk at the lawn party most of the time," acknowledged TeleCable director of engineering Nick Worth. "It took a lot of patience, a lot of risk-taking and some tough years."[13]

TeleCable's strategy was to concentrate on getting franchises and building its own systems, rather than buying going concerns. In this way, it could get a quick return of capital, while at the same time building valuable cable systems.

With the purchase of the North Carolina newspapers in 1965 and the continued expansion of TeleCable, it was time to change the company's name from Norfolk-Portsmouth Newspapers. George J. Hebert, an editorial page editor for the *Ledger-Star,* suggested Landmark.[14] The *Norfolk Landmark* had been among the forebears of the modern *Pilot.* Founded in 1873, it had been one of the city's several morning dailies before a series of mergers and acquisitions had melded it with the *Norfolk Virginian,* then the *Daily Pilot,* to create the modern paper. On February 3, 1967, the company officially was named Landmark Communications, Inc.

By the early 1970s, U.S. cable operators had wired most of the small towns and cities where broadcast TV signals were weak. Tele-Cable built systems in Selma, Decatur, and Auburn/Opelika, Alabama; Wytheville, Virginia; Racine, Wisconsin; Kokomo, Indiana; Columbus, Georgia; and Bloomington, Illinois.

At the behest of worried network television broadcasters, the Federal Communications Commission prohibited cable systems from importing distant signals and limited their ability to offer movies, sporting events, and syndicated programming. The result: financing for new system construction dried up. The FCC eventually relented, and TeleCable built new systems in Overland Park, Kansas, and Spartanburg, South Carolina, markets in which broadcast reception was good. Persuading residents in suburban Kansas City to pay for the same TV signals they received off their antennas

was a tough sell, even after TeleCable of Overland Park added locally produced programming. Penetration in these urban markets
was low. Losses mounted.

The event that would transform the cable TV industry to mass
medium was the development of powerful, synchronous satellites
that made possible the reception of television signals by small antennas, just five to ten meters in diameter. Cable TV operators across
America began installing satellite-receiving dishes and offered
the service to their subscribers. Ted Turner's Atlanta TV station,
WTBS, soon followed HBO, ESPN, USA, Nickelodeon, Showtime,
and the Movie Channel to fill the RCA Satcom satellite. TeleCable
was the first multisystem cable operator, or MSO, owner to install
satellite dishes to all its subscribers.

The advent of programming services delivered by satellite would
spur a new, more intense round of franchising. Competition was
fierce. The cable gold rush lasted for about a decade. During that
period there was "all kinds of skullduggery," Batten said, partly because cable's existence was decided by local governments and there
was a temptation for people to cheat to get the franchises.

One method of swaying votes was known as "rent a citizen." A
cable company determined who the political heavyweights were in
a town where a franchise was to be awarded. They then "rented" the
powerbrokers' influence in return for gifts of stock, which sometimes
amounted to as much as 20 percent of a cable company. In return, the
community leaders delivered city council's votes for the franchise. It
was all legal, but Batten viewed the approach as unscrupulous.

Trying to compete for franchises was frustrating to TeleCable
managers. "We got hammered two or three times by groups where
we thought they had inferior proposals,"[15] recalled Page Lea, a member of the franchising team. In many respects, cable was not so much
a business as it was a political play, said E. C. "Barney" Oldfield Jr.,
TeleCable's vice president of franchising. "We had a terrific track
record. But here we get thrown into this cauldron of lies and deceit
and innuendo."[16]

Eventually, Batten agreed to sell, but not give away, TeleCable stock. Local investors were required to put in their fair share of equity so they'd have as much at risk in the venture as TeleCable. Despite a sometimes uneven playing field, TeleCable got its share of the business. When franchising was at a fever pitch, Batten calmly told Roberts, "Dick, I want to win and I expect you guys to win your share of franchises. But never do anything under the table even if that means we don't win a single franchise."[17]

"I cannot describe to you how empowering that was to us,"[18] said Roberts, who became president of TeleCable in 1977. When the company won a franchise, "folks knew that we had won fair and square," said Gordon Herring, TeleCable's executive vice president. "When we lost, we walked away as gentlemen."

TeleCable added Lexington, Kentucky; Springfield, Missouri; Greenville County, South Carolina; and Arlington, Richardson, and Plano, Texas. It purchased partially built systems in Cleveland, Tennessee, and Broward County, Florida. It expanded all of its existing properties.

TeleCable was a pioneer in engineering, marketing, and advertising. It was the first to develop multiplexing, a concept that offered cable customers a network with multiple channels at no additional cost. TeleCable was one of the first in the industry to offer fully addressable converters and high-tech predictive dialing call centers, a highly powerful marketing tool. With the software built into the small black cable converter boxes planted on top of television sets, customers could add a premium service such as HBO without having to leave home.

TeleCable also was a leader in ad sales revenue generation. Most cable companies saw advertising as an ancillary service of its cable systems. TeleCable had the advantage of advertising know-how from Batten's newspapers and TV and radio stations. Most other cable companies did not have the capability of inserting advertising,[19] and instead covered the local spots with public service announcements. TeleCable further invested in the automated technology to produce and run the commercials and a production department to create the ads.

According to Jim Robbins, president and CEO of Cox Communications until his retirement in 2005, the cable industry in its infancy was a "ragtag collection of pole climbers and former TV repair people." TeleCable brought professional management, good business values, and forward-looking business practices "as opposed to pure opportunists."[20]

As vice president of affiliate sales for HBO, Gail Sermersheim's job was to get cable companies to carry HBO on its programming lineup at the lowest possible cost to the network; the cable companies in turn tried to get as much money from the networks as they could. It didn't work that way with Batten's company. TeleCable had a philosophy of developing win-win situations, she said. "It's an example of how you can run a company exceedingly well and be profitable and highly successful and still be respectful of all your employees, suppliers, and business peers." At TeleCable, "no one was ever knifing anyone in the back, there were no harsh words about someone else," she said. "Everyone was on the same page, which meant good leadership."[21]

In 1984, by then the nation's fourteenth-largest cable company, TeleCable was spun off from Landmark as a separate corporation. In 1995, Batten sold the company for $1.5 billion to John Malone's TeleCommunications Inc., which at the time was the country's largest cable company.

In 1968, only three years after borrowing $10 million to buy the Greensboro newspapers, Batten paid off the note in full and mulled his next opportunity. He had heard rumors that western Virginia's largest daily papers, the *Roanoke Times* and its afternoon sister, the *World-News*, might go on the block. The Times-World Corporation, some 200 miles west of Norfolk, also included the weekly *Galax Gazette*, CBS affiliate WDBJ-TV, AM and FM radio stations, and a shopping center.

Framed by the Blue Ridge Mountains, Roanoke has a tough Appalachian work ethic, and it has long been a community of newspaper junkies: in 2002 and 2006, a greater percentage of local adults

The owners of Norfolk-Portsmouth Newspapers Inc. have a capacity for continuing dynamic growth and a willingness to accept new challenges. They also have a determination to carry out any mission to which they dedicate their heart, mind and hand. They have a healthy ambition, becoming modesty and a modern outlook. They are abreast of changes in the communications field and alert to capitalize on them. They are keenly interested in public affairs and recognize the important role of communication in the life of the 20th century. The best way to gauge their standards is to examine the excellent quality of their product in Norfolk.[5]

Batten published a statement the same day. He assured readers that the newspapers' executives would be autonomous and that they would live in Greensboro, although oversight of WFMY-TV would shift to Norfolk. He pledged that both the newspapers and the TV station would be dedicated to public service.

The Greensboro properties were Batten's first acquisition after his uncle's death, and the debt was substantial. Batten had convinced the Colonel to spend $1 million for the *Portsmouth Star* in 1955, but the Greensboro properties required $5 million from the company's savings and another more than $10 million in bank loans, including $600,000 in annual installments and, after ten years, a $4.6 million balloon payment.[6] Colleagues were surprised that Batten was willing to take on the Greensboro debt, but he was convinced he could turn the unprofitable company around.

With the Greensboro newspapers operating in the red, it was obvious to Batten that new management was sorely needed. Batten named himself president of the newspapers and the television station; Paul Huber was appointed a vice president. Peter B. Bush, advertising director for the Norfolk newspapers, moved to Greensboro as general manager. Dick Hendricks, who had been the controller for the newspapers in Norfolk, went as assistant general manager the following year. Carl Jeffress was kept on as publisher and a director while William Saunders, the sales promotion manager for Sears,

Roebuck and Co. in Norfolk, who'd started his career in the *Pilot*'s advertising department, became ad director.

When Kenneth W. Baldwin Jr. arrived in Greensboro as the new personnel chief, the newspapers had no such office. He created detailed files. He developed hiring standards that included reference checks. A battery of tests were administered throughout the company. In production, for example, workers were quizzed on their mechanical, comprehension, and general aptitude skills. That led in some cases to employees in journeymen jobs becoming supervisors.

Batten announced that Norfolk's pension plan was being implemented in Greensboro. Workers would be given credit for their years of employment as if they always had been part of the plan. The benefit represented a $12 million to $13 million liability. Still, employees were suspicious. Batten wasn't a Carolinian, and some of the newspapers' managers lamented that "some foreigner from Virginia" had bought the papers.

The newspapers' physical plant had been neglected. The three-story brick building was dark and dirty. The heat and air conditioning barely worked. Sheet metal patched weak sections of the wooden floors. The equipment was antiquated. In Batten's view, the newspapers also suffered from what he called "wall-to-wall" unions. He considered it an insult to have unions between him and his employees.

To modernize the "back shop"—where workers setting type, printing, assembling, and bundling newspapers used outmoded equipment that required slow, tedious labor—jobs had to be eliminated. The unions threatened to strike.

Production was transitioning from ages-old hot lead typesetting to a new technology—photographic, or "cold," type—and the department's several hundred workers resisted the change and their coveted union-won comforts. In case the unions staged a walkout, senior managers taught non-union workers to operate the presses. Preparations were made to hire permanent back shop replacements. Several executives were sent to out-of-state "scab school" where they were trained to produce the paper with skeleton staffing.

The union-management relationship was so tenuous at some newspapers in the 1960s and 1970s that armed guards were necessary to keep the peace. But the union bosses in Greensboro never made good on their threats to strike. They held informational pickets to let the public know they were unhappy, and there was occasional verbal harassment, but there was no violence. In the end, unions left the Greensboro news operation without a stoppage, and the modernizing continued.[7] There never has been a strike at any of Batten's more than 100 daily and community newspapers.

Batten's friend Kay Graham wasn't so lucky. A five-month walkout by *Washington Post* unions had traumatized her management team. As with Greensboro, the *Post* was intent on eliminating redundant staff and procedures it felt threatened the paper's fiscal health. Contracts with nine of the *Post*'s unions expired on October 1, 1975. At 4 a.m. that day, after disabling fire extinguishers, *Post* pressmen set fire to one of the newspaper's nine presses. They ripped out electrical wiring and operating parts, stripped gears, and slashed newsprint rolls on the nine presses' seventy-two printing units. The pressroom foreman was severely beaten. Joined by the other craft unions, the pressmen walked out. The Newspaper Guild, incensed by the damage, refused to honor the picket line and kept working.[8]

Batten and Stan Cook of the *Chicago Tribune* visited Graham periodically to offer advice about handling the showdown.[9] After dinner in her Georgetown home one evening, Batten said he would send five *Virginian-Pilot* production employees to help repair *Post* presses. R. G. "Bud" Dashiell, the *Pilot*'s mechanical superintendent, was asked to supervise the electrical repair work. Dashiell was airlifted by helicopter to the roof of the *Post* to avoid potential violence at the picket line and stayed three weeks to repair damage.[10]

In 1964, prior to the purchase of the Greensboro newspapers, Batten had already taken the first steps to expand his business into an entirely different medium. That year, Batten's Norfolk-Portsmouth Newspapers Inc. paid $15,000 for the television cable franchise in tiny Roanoke Rapids, North Carolina, eighty-five miles southwest of Norfolk.[11] Cable television was at that time a necessity for viewers in rural areas. Too far from broadcast towers to receive strong signals, they faced limited or poor reception that could be reduced to impenetrable in bad weather. In Roanoke Rapids, TV reception was so bad that most house roofs sported twenty-to-thirty-foot poles with antennas and rotors. If residents wanted to view a station out of Raleigh, the antenna was turned one way, another for Richmond, and still another for Norfolk. Even then the TV picture was snowy.

The cable business was fairly simple, with potentially excellent returns. Municipalities sought bids from cable companies and typically awarded a fifteen-year franchise to the system operator they deemed best for their communities. The cable operator built a "head end"—antennas to receive distant signals and modulate them onto coaxial cables—strung the cables on telephone or power poles, and connected the lines to homes. Batten was drawn to cable's uncomplicated technology, and he was convinced that marketing one type of subscription was not unlike marketing another. At about the same time that he bought the Roanoke Rapids franchise, Batten okayed $12,000, or one dollar per household, to buy the Beckley, West Virginia, franchise and $6,000 to buy one in Princeton, West Virginia. Building systems for each community drove the costs up; the initial investment in Roanoke Rapids was roughly $500,000.

Batten put together a small team in Norfolk and, marrying "television" with "cable," named the new business TeleCable. He hired Rex Bradley, whom he had met at Harvard Business School, to run it. Dick Roberts, who had worked in the *Virginian-Pilot*'s marketing research department, became vice president of operations. TeleCable was designed to be what its managers called a cost-containing "loose-tight" organization.[12] Programming, engineering, human resources, and marketing departments were centralized in Norfolk. Each local manager, however, was empowered to hire and fire and make other key decisions.

TeleCable was a business that required patience and a willingness to invest in the future. It produced large tax losses through the accelerated depreciation of its construction costs. The parent company wrote off the losses immediately against its newspaper and TV profits, and since the business was a private company, there was little concern about recording big book losses.

Publishers at Batten's newspapers were skeptical about the new business. "We were the skunk at the lawn party most of the time," acknowledged TeleCable director of engineering Nick Worth. "It took a lot of patience, a lot of risk-taking and some tough years."[13]

TeleCable's strategy was to concentrate on getting franchises and building its own systems, rather than buying going concerns. In this way, it could get a quick return of capital, while at the same time building valuable cable systems.

With the purchase of the North Carolina newspapers in 1965 and the continued expansion of TeleCable, it was time to change the company's name from Norfolk-Portsmouth Newspapers. George J. Hebert, an editorial page editor for the *Ledger-Star,* suggested Landmark.[14] The *Norfolk Landmark* had been among the forebears of the modern *Pilot.* Founded in 1873, it had been one of the city's several morning dailies before a series of mergers and acquisitions had melded it with the *Norfolk Virginian,* then the *Daily Pilot,* to create the modern paper. On February 3, 1967, the company officially was named Landmark Communications, Inc.

By the early 1970s, U.S. cable operators had wired most of the small towns and cities where broadcast TV signals were weak. Tele-Cable built systems in Selma, Decatur, and Auburn/Opelika, Alabama; Wytheville, Virginia; Racine, Wisconsin; Kokomo, Indiana; Columbus, Georgia; and Bloomington, Illinois.

At the behest of worried network television broadcasters, the Federal Communications Commission prohibited cable systems from importing distant signals and limited their ability to offer movies, sporting events, and syndicated programming. The result: financing for new system construction dried up. The FCC eventually relented, and TeleCable built new systems in Overland Park, Kansas, and Spartanburg, South Carolina, markets in which broadcast reception was good. Persuading residents in suburban Kansas City to pay for the same TV signals they received off their antennas

was a tough sell, even after TeleCable of Overland Park added locally produced programming. Penetration in these urban markets
was low. Losses mounted.

The event that would transform the cable TV industry to mass
medium was the development of powerful, synchronous satellites
that made possible the reception of television signals by small antennas, just five to ten meters in diameter. Cable TV operators across
America began installing satellite-receiving dishes and offered
the service to their subscribers. Ted Turner's Atlanta TV station,
WTBS, soon followed HBO, ESPN, USA, Nickelodeon, Showtime,
and the Movie Channel to fill the RCA Satcom satellite. TeleCable
was the first multisystem cable operator, or MSO, owner to install
satellite dishes to all its subscribers.

The advent of programming services delivered by satellite would
spur a new, more intense round of franchising. Competition was
fierce. The cable gold rush lasted for about a decade. During that
period there was "all kinds of skullduggery," Batten said, partly because cable's existence was decided by local governments and there
was a temptation for people to cheat to get the franchises.

One method of swaying votes was known as "rent a citizen." A
cable company determined who the political heavyweights were in
a town where a franchise was to be awarded. They then "rented" the
powerbrokers' influence in return for gifts of stock, which sometimes
amounted to as much as 20 percent of a cable company. In return, the
community leaders delivered city council's votes for the franchise. It
was all legal, but Batten viewed the approach as unscrupulous.

Trying to compete for franchises was frustrating to TeleCable
managers. "We got hammered two or three times by groups where
we thought they had inferior proposals,"[15] recalled Page Lea, a member of the franchising team. In many respects, cable was not so much
a business as it was a political play, said E. C. "Barney" Oldfield Jr.,
TeleCable's vice president of franchising. "We had a terrific track
record. But here we get thrown into this cauldron of lies and deceit
and innuendo."[16]

Eventually, Batten agreed to sell, but not give away, TeleCable stock. Local investors were required to put in their fair share of equity so they'd have as much at risk in the venture as TeleCable. Despite a sometimes uneven playing field, TeleCable got its share of the business. When franchising was at a fever pitch, Batten calmly told Roberts, "Dick, I want to win and I expect you guys to win your share of franchises. But never do anything under the table even if that means we don't win a single franchise."[17]

"I cannot describe to you how empowering that was to us,"[18] said Roberts, who became president of TeleCable in 1977. When the company won a franchise, "folks knew that we had won fair and square," said Gordon Herring, TeleCable's executive vice president. "When we lost, we walked away as gentlemen."

TeleCable added Lexington, Kentucky; Springfield, Missouri; Greenville County, South Carolina; and Arlington, Richardson, and Plano, Texas. It purchased partially built systems in Cleveland, Tennessee, and Broward County, Florida. It expanded all of its existing properties.

TeleCable was a pioneer in engineering, marketing, and advertising. It was the first to develop multiplexing, a concept that offered cable customers a network with multiple channels at no additional cost. TeleCable was one of the first in the industry to offer fully addressable converters and high-tech predictive dialing call centers, a highly powerful marketing tool. With the software built into the small black cable converter boxes planted on top of television sets, customers could add a premium service such as HBO without having to leave home.

TeleCable also was a leader in ad sales revenue generation. Most cable companies saw advertising as an ancillary service of its cable systems. TeleCable had the advantage of advertising know-how from Batten's newspapers and TV and radio stations. Most other cable companies did not have the capability of inserting advertising,[19] and instead covered the local spots with public service announcements. TeleCable further invested in the automated technology to produce and run the commercials and a production department to create the ads.

According to Jim Robbins, president and CEO of Cox Communications until his retirement in 2005, the cable industry in its infancy was a "ragtag collection of pole climbers and former TV repair people." TeleCable brought professional management, good business values, and forward-looking business practices "as opposed to pure opportunists."[20]

As vice president of affiliate sales for HBO, Gail Sermersheim's job was to get cable companies to carry HBO on its programming lineup at the lowest possible cost to the network; the cable companies in turn tried to get as much money from the networks as they could. It didn't work that way with Batten's company. TeleCable had a philosophy of developing win-win situations, she said. "It's an example of how you can run a company exceedingly well and be profitable and highly successful and still be respectful of all your employees, suppliers, and business peers." At TeleCable, "no one was ever knifing anyone in the back, there were no harsh words about someone else," she said. "Everyone was on the same page, which meant good leadership."[21]

In 1984, by then the nation's fourteenth-largest cable company, TeleCable was spun off from Landmark as a separate corporation. In 1995, Batten sold the company for $1.5 billion to John Malone's TeleCommunications Inc., which at the time was the country's largest cable company.

In 1968, only three years after borrowing $10 million to buy the Greensboro newspapers, Batten paid off the note in full and mulled his next opportunity. He had heard rumors that western Virginia's largest daily papers, the *Roanoke Times* and its afternoon sister, the *World-News*, might go on the block. The Times-World Corporation, some 200 miles west of Norfolk, also included the weekly *Galax Gazette*, CBS affiliate WDBJ-TV, AM and FM radio stations, and a shopping center.

Framed by the Blue Ridge Mountains, Roanoke has a tough Appalachian work ethic, and it has long been a community of newspaper junkies: in 2002 and 2006, a greater percentage of local adults read the *Roanoke Times* than any other daily newspaper in the country. It consistently remains in the top ten nationally for readership.

The family-owned company appealed to Batten. The *Roanoke Daily Times* had debuted in 1886 to serve the up-and-coming railroad town, once known as Big Lick. In 1909, a group of businessmen led by Roanoke banker J. B. Fishburn bought the *Times* and the *Evening News*. Four years later, they added the *Evening World* and renamed the afternoon paper the *World-News*. In 1918, the Fishburn family acquired majority ownership of the newspapers and made a gift of the Times-World Corporation to J.B.'s son, Junius. He stepped down as president of the newspapers in January 1954 with plans to remain active in the company. Succeeding him was M. William "Bill" Armistead III.

Fishburn unexpectedly died three months later, and the First National Exchange Bank became trustee of the newspapers' holdings. Armistead remained in charge of day-to-day operations. Bob Fishburn tried to follow in his late father's footsteps. He was hired as a reporter but didn't have the instincts for the job. He sold advertising for Times-World's TV station. It was a disaster, he said. He realized he wasn't cut out to be an executive and signed on as an editorial writer. He loved it.

A strained relationship with Armistead eroded any lingering thoughts Fishburn might have given to succeeding his father in the business. Troubled by the newspapers' whites-only wedding announcement policy, Fishburn dashed off a note to Armistead expressing his frustration with the edict. "What the hell," he thought, "I'm a stockholder." He was called into Armistead's office, along with Barton W. Morris, the *Times*'s executive editor. Ignoring Fishburn, Armistead turned to Morris. "Barton, tell this young whippersnapper that if he ever writes another note like that, he's fired."[22]

Fishburn walked out of Armistead's office and telephoned his sister. "Sally, he threatened to fire me," he would recall telling her. "I think if we put our stocks together, we could fire him." Both men thought better of their behavior. Fishburn backed off, and within months, the newspaper began running wedding announcements for African American brides.

After considerable market research and aware that there was no apparent family heir, Batten was ready to make an offer. In a development reminiscent of Greensboro, the family changed its mind. Armistead knew Frank Batten to be a straight shooter who ran a good newspaper. If and when the Fishburns decided to sell, he told Batten he'd let him know.

In the summer of 1968, Knight Newspapers Inc., the forerunner of Knight Ridder, went to the Times-World board of directors with an attractive offer. Keeping his word, Armistead flew to Norfolk to talk with Batten. "We have an offer on the table," he said. "Come up with what you can and we will decide who gets it."[23]

Batten would have to sell the TV station if he won the bid because of federal requirements forbidding overlapping coverage of WDBJ-TV in Roanoke and WFMY-TV, Landmark's station in Greensboro. The radio stations also would be sold. And Batten certainly had no use for the Towers Shopping Center, even though it occupied a premier location in what was then suburban Roanoke. Times-World had bought the property to erect its radio tower and leased the unused acreage to a developer who built retail stores. After the shopping center's owner went belly-up, Times-World bought the buildings at auction and found itself in the commercial real estate business. Batten offered a total of $19 million for the Times-World Corporation, beating out Knight Newspapers' bid.

WDBJ-TV was sold to Schurz Communications of South Bend, Indiana. The AM radio station was bought by the Vodrey family of East Liverpool, Ohio. The FM channel was sold to Jim Gibbons, the radio voice of the Redskins football team. Hunter Hogan, Batten's father-in-law, had developed the shopping center and was still its leasing agent. Hogan put together a syndicate that bought the shopping center, and in November 1969 Batten added the Roanoke newspapers to his growing enterprise.

One of his first decrees was to get rid of company cars. He didn't want the fringe benefits to become a standard at his other newspapers and sold the vehicles to the managers who had been using them. The companies that had the most frills tended to be the companies he respected the least. He viewed such excess as a reflection of how they were managed. As with the corporate offices in Norfolk, there would be no extravagances, no outlandish spending, and no unnecessary frills.

He wasn't solely about saving money. Walter Rugaber, president and publisher of the *Roanoke Times* from 1982 to 2000, conferred with Batten about choosing the location for an annual Landmark newspaper managers' gathering. With both Roanoke and Greensboro hours away from Norfolk, it was difficult to find a central meeting spot that was easily accessible.

Rugaber found that the Homestead Resort, a grand hotel operating since 1766 in the mountains about seventy-five miles from Roanoke, would cost less than another hotel the company was considering. Batten told Rugaber, "Well, you know, it would never be understood if we went off to the Homestead." The resort's grandeur might be seen as coddling by the workforce, as profligate spending. And that wasn't his way.[24]

The one indulgence Batten did allow himself and his senior managers was the Beechcraft airplane that came with the Roanoke papers. With commercial flights from Norfolk to outlying papers requiring as many as four layovers, the Beechcraft was more of a necessity than a luxury. "I'm not going to make up a lot of bullshit statements that this was critical to the success of the company," Batten later said, "but it made life a lot easier for the managers who had to commute to those places."

As Batten developed his business in the 1960s, he continued to expand his community presence as well. He was president of the Norfolk area Chamber of Commerce and chaired the United Way drive. But few themes in Frank Batten's adult life were as consistently well defined as the value he placed on education. In 1962 he was instrumental in the establishment of a new college in Norfolk.

In the decade after World War II, the number of students attending the city's public schools nearly quadrupled to 84,000. Yet those students were served by only a junior college, established as a division of the College of William and Mary in 1930. In March 1960, the Virginia General Assembly officially changed the state-funded college's name to the Colleges of William and Mary, which now included the main Williamsburg campus, satellites in Norfolk and Richmond, and junior colleges in Newport News and Petersburg. With policies for the offshoot campuses set forty-five miles away in Williamsburg, Norfolk Division director, Lewis W. Webb Jr., appointed a twelve-person advisory board for the Norfolk campus to push for local control. As one of its members, Batten helped lobby state and elected officials to transform the school into an independent college with its own local identification.

When the Virginia General Assembly passed legislation to make this a reality in 1962, Batten was appointed as the new college's first rector. He was thirty-five. After trying to find a name for the new school that was appropriate to the area (suggestions included Regal College of Norfolk, Thomas Jefferson College, and College of the Atlantic), the Board of Visitors chose the name "Old Dominion," the nickname given to the Commonwealth of Virginia by King Charles II in 1660. Old Dominion College became Old Dominion University in 1969.

Batten would serve two terms as rector. In the summer of 1973, his last as an ODU board member, he spoke at the school's commencement. It was remarkable that the university had come so far, he told them, noting that the institution would never achieve its potential until Virginia provided it with the resources to do the job. It was time for the new graduates to develop political muscle to influence the future of Old Dominion. He challenged them to become a powerful voice for their alma mater. After eleven years on its board, he resigned to accept an appointment to the State Council of Higher Education, where he'd be in a better position to bird-dog support for the school.

Virginia politicians, ever vigilant for candidates with name recognition, status, and money, courted Batten. He was urged to run for Congress. Friends encouraged him to run for governor of Virginia, and he briefly toyed with the idea. He would have enjoyed some aspects of being governor, particularly being in a position to influence the future of education in Virginia. "But there were a lot of things I would have hated," he concluded, such as "all the political maneuverings, all the people you'd have to cotton up to."

He chose to stay on the periphery of politics, backing friends like William B. Spong Jr., who was elected to the U.S. Senate in 1966, and William C. Battle, who lost his gubernatorial bid in 1969. Both were Democrats. Batten considered himself a moderate and did not align himself with either major political party. Over the years he would vote for Republican presidents Eisenhower and George Bush, and for candidate John McCain, and he supported Democratic Virginia governors Mark Warner and Tim Kaine.

He would continue to make his mark and consolidate his power in other ways. On September 1, 1967, eight years after her husband's death, Fay Slover, eighty-three, died after a long illness. Batten had been prepared for his aunt's death; he had been stunned by his sixty-year-old mother's death of a heart attack three years earlier. With his aunt, uncle, and mother gone, Batten now was in sole control of the company.

10 Legal Challenges

T HE INVOLVEMENT of the media in the community led to some difficult legal challenges for Landmark in the late 1960s and early 1970s. Batten still shared command of the Norfolk newspapers, he as publisher and Paul Huber Jr. as president. They had known each other since childhood because of the close working relationship between Slover and Huber's father, Paul Sr., the former president of the newspapers.

In 1954, when the Colonel installed his nephew as publisher, he'd appointed Paul Jr. as president, partly to pay homage to the elder Huber, who had died eight years earlier. Huber remained president after Batten gave his company the Landmark name and took on the role of chairman of the board.

Landmark's top executives were encouraged to take active roles in the community and as president of Landmark, Paul Huber Jr. served on various local boards, including the Norfolk Savings & Loan Corporation. It was Virginia's largest uninsured industrial loan company, with a state charter dating to the end of World War I. Huber had been a director since 1953.

Without the board's knowledge, Norfolk Savings & Loan's president and vice president had been skimming cash from deposits for a decade—among their targets 416 Christmas Savings Club accounts.[1] The firm began to lose money as early as 1959 and was insolvent by 1963, but it wasn't until July 1972 that State Corporation Commission auditors discovered that its books didn't balance and that the company could not cover deposits. Huber and the other directors claimed they had been in the dark about the improprieties. Outside auditors hired by the firm said they also had been smoke screened.

To recoup the money, the corporation began liquidating its assets, selling loans at a discount to Virginia National Bank. It was too little, too late. In January 1973, the state shut down the savings and loan. Locked out were more than 3,500 depositors who'd mistakenly assumed that their nest eggs, a collective $12.3 million, were secure and federally insured.

The courts named Edwin R. MacKethan, a lawyer and retired banker, as receiver for the defunct business. His job was to try to corral as much of the depositors' lost cash as possible. He filed ten multimillion-dollar lawsuits on the depositors' behalf.

MacKethan blamed former Norfolk First Citizen Daniel M. Thornton for the scheme that led to the firm's collapse. Thornton, who died in 1970, was the savings and loan's president and chairman. In a deposition, Leon C. Hall, who succeeded Thornton as president, admitted that he withheld a critical audit from directors two years before the firm's collapse on instructions from Thornton. MacKethan alleged that Thornton had set up "straw" corporations to hide bad loans from directors and state bank examiners.

The following year, Hall was sentenced to seven years in prison on federal mail fraud and conspiracy charges. A former Norfolk Savings vice president got four years on similar charges. Both men were paroled after serving about seventeen months, then were returned to jail on state embezzlement charges.[2]

At the same time the criminal cases were in the courts, lawsuits were filed against three former directors, including Huber, and two Norfolk Savings lawyers. In April 1974, MacKethan filed $22 million civil suits against Landmark Communications; Peat, Marwick, Mitchell & Company, the S&L's accounting firm; and Virginia National Bank.

According to the lawsuits, accountants knew in 1968 that there was corruption afoot, but withheld the report for more than a year; the bank controlled the insolvent savings and loan as far back as the 1950s; and Paul Huber had learned of the firm's illegal practices and insolvency in 1967, had done nothing to correct them, and had continued to permit the newspapers to sell advertising to Norfolk Savings, duping new depositors.

Batten believed that Huber, who did not oversee the newspapers' advertising or news content, could not be held responsible for a financial institution's newspaper ads. Batten contended that the only reason Landmark was sued was that the receiver was hunting for deep pockets.[3]

On April 20, 1974, a week after Landmark was sued, Batten promoted Bill Armistead to president and chief operating officer. Huber was named Landmark's vice chairman, removing him from day-to-day operations.

In January 1975, a U.S. District Court judge granted Landmark a partial summary judgment in ruling that the federal court would refuse to hear any issues where only state law applied. The judge said MacKethan could not collect $11 million in punitive damages that had been requested as part of the original $22 million lawsuit, thus limiting the maximum award to Norfolk Savings' approximate losses.

The trial against Landmark began later that month in Alexandria, Virginia. Huber testified that he was unaware of any improprieties at the savings and loan until July 1972, when State Banking Commissioner Thomas D. Jones filed his report. Jones reportedly then recommended that the directors keep the institution operating and continue accepting new deposits.

Lawyers for Landmark argued that Huber and the S&L's other directors were innocent victims of the president's chicanery. Huber's duties at Landmark were downplayed. "Frank Batten, the true operating head of Landmark, never encouraged Huber to join Norfolk Savings's board and was never told even what Huber knew about Norfolk Savings's developing problems," the jury was told. And even if Huber had known, he had succeeded his father on the board and served in a purely private capacity—not in his role as a Landmark executive.[4]

Lawyers for the depositors contended that Huber admitted to knowing enough about the savings and loan's financial instability to show that false advertising was printed and broadcast. Regardless of his job description at Landmark, it was his responsibility to halt advertising that suggested the firm was stable. And he was an agent of Landmark, the lawyers claimed, in that he promoted Landmark's advertising revenue or lent Landmark's prestige to Norfolk Savings.

Batten was the final witness in the six-day trial. He testified that he learned from Huber in late December 1972 that Norfolk Savings would be closed by state authorities on January 2, 1973. A Norfolk Savings ad for depositors was printed in the newspaper during the intervening period. Batten said he was only vaguely aware that Norfolk Savings & Loan was advertising in the newspapers. It never occurred to him, he told the jury, that "they'd be dumb enough to advertise anywhere after they were closing down."[5]

On February 5, 1975, the four-man, two-woman jury handed down a $2 million verdict against Landmark. Remarked one of the jurors: "We felt that Huber didn't know anything until July 12, 1972, but that after that, he knew. He was president of Landmark. We felt that he should have put what he knew in his newspaper."[6] On Valentine's Day, another jury before the same judge awarded Norfolk Savings' receiver a $4 million judgment against Virginia National Bank.

In a February memorandum, Landmark contended that if its newspapers had published news stories that Norfolk Savings was insolvent, there would have been an immediate run on the corporation, forcing it to close with all the losses to depositors and creditors that ultimately occurred less than six months later.[7] Landmark asked that the verdict be set aside or that a new trial be ordered. But the following month, Landmark and Virginia National Bank—along with Huber and five other Norfolk Savings directors against whom the receiver had a pending lawsuit—settled out of court, agreeing to pay a total of $6.6 million.[8]

Although the judgment had been unfair in Batten's eyes, he felt he had no choice but to ask for Huber's resignation. It would have been a strike against Landmark for Huber to stay on as president, he said. And to ignore Huber's responsibility for Landmark's $2 million liability would have been unfair to the company's executive stockholders.[9]

Before leaving on March 18, 1975, Huber sold his 13 percent interest in Landmark, valued at $2.15 million, and contributed the proceeds to the settlement. Landmark paid an additional $1.35 million and Virginia National Bank, $3.1 million. Had her husband known anything about Norfolk Savings' fraudulent activities, he never would have allowed it to go on, said Sarah Huber, whose husband died in 1998. "The hardest part of this whole situation was not the money," she said. "It was that he was lied to and misled by Thornton."[10]

While the Norfolk Savings & Loan case was being pursued, Batten was also addressing a challenge to his Federal Communications Commission license for WTAR-TV in Norfolk, an affiliate of CBS, the first station to have a full-time correspondent at the state capitol during Virginia General Assembly sessions and the first in Virginia to use a helicopter for traffic reports.

Norfolk Newspapers had no competition for the WTAR-TV license and put the station on the air in April 1950. Television was thought so risky at the time that WTAR's three-story brick building, constructed across the alley from the Norfolk newspapers, was designed to be converted into offices if the new technology flopped. The FCC regulates television, cable, radio, wireless, and satellite and issues broadcast licenses, which must be renewed every eight years, three at the time of the challenge. While most renewals are routine, all licenses are subject to public scrutiny and possible revocation.

A challenge to the license of a Mississippi television station by the United Church of Christ and two black Mississippians in 1964, claiming that WLBT-TV in Jackson had failed to give fair coverage to civil rights and integration issues, established the precedent that the public could participate in FCC decisions. It also pushed broadcasters to hire more minorities and provide fairer coverage of minorities.[11] Other broadcast licenses began to face opposition. In January 1969, the FCC awarded a license to a competing applicant in Boston, triggering a nationwide push to unseat existing company licenses, including Norfolk's.

In September 1969, Hampton Roads Television Corporation, established by Norfolk lawyer Gordon E. Campbell and Republican

District Committee Chairman Wayne E. Lustig, challenged the WTAR-TV license, which was set to expire the following month.

It was the first time WTAR had faced a renewal challenge and the first time anyone had questioned its permit.[12] After more than two years of delays, the FCC in May 1972 began the WTAR hearing in Washington. Hampton Roads Television sought to disqualify WTAR-TV as an applicant because of prohibited cross-interests with local stations WAVY-TV and WVEC-TV. Because Batten owned stock in local TV stations while also serving on the board of Virginia National Bank, it was claimed that Landmark could not be objective in covering the bank's activities.

Batten denied allegations that there was any policy at his newspapers and broadcast stations to withhold adverse information about the bank because he was a VNB director and stockholder. "If I knew of any instance in which that happened, I would fire the editor," Batten testified.[13]

The hearing continued through most of June, complicated by a U.S. Circuit Court of Appeals ruling the previous year requiring that potential new licensees be given full consideration, regardless of the past service of the incumbent. Previously, the license holder had been assumed to be virtually unassailable if shown to have given substantial service to the public. WTAR president Lee Kitchin filed a forty-page affidavit showing services the station provided for the Norfolk area. Charges and countercharges flew for days on issues ranging from whether the station should broadcast editorials, to an allegation that Batten instructed a former WTAR news director to reduce news coverage of a Norfolk lawyer and local government critic. Batten denied the claims. His lawyer pointed out that not only had the news director been fired from WTAR, but he was now a minority stockholder and potential news director for Hampton Roads Television.[14]

On August 1, the FCC proceedings moved to Norfolk. State Senator Peter K. Babalas testified that Landmark "controls the pulse and the heartbeat of Norfolk."[15] Lawyer Frederick "Bingo" Stant Jr.

claimed that his 1968 campaign for Congress was destroyed by the "drumbeat and drumfire" of WTAR.[16] Other community leaders spoke for and against Landmark's ownership of the station during twenty-four days of testimony. On March 21, 1973, FCC administrative law judge David I. Kraushaar ruled in favor of WTAR.

The relief was short-lived. WTAR's Kitchin left Norfolk in 1973 to lead the Times-World Corporation in Roanoke and was replaced at the station by William A. Gietz. Hampton Roads Television leveled a new claim against Landmark: that WTAR-TV replaced Kitchin without proper FCC notification in an attempt to conceal its plans for a change in leadership. In August 1974, the ruling in favor of WTAR and Landmark was set aside.

Hearings reopened in November. Edgar W. Holtz, Landmark's Washington lawyer, testified that he had advised Batten that the change in WTAR presidents would have no adverse effect on the FCC case. He also told Batten that Hampton Roads TV might try to reopen the case.

In January 1975, Judge Kraushaar dismissed the challenge as too minor for consideration, pointing to the "solid experience in journalism and broadcasting" of the station's owners. WTAR "has a built-in source from which to draw experienced personnel, some of whom . . . may be minor nonvoting shareholders," the judge wrote, "but the real power in the corporation is Mr. Frank Batten, chairman of the board of both WTAR-TV and Landmark." Kraushaar praised Batten's "complete candor and honesty."[17]

Ten months later, in October 1975, as Landmark awaited full FCC board approval, the federal agency again reopened the challenge. Hampton Roads Television this time questioned Landmark's corporate character in the wake of the $2 million jury verdict against the company in the recently finished Norfolk Savings & Loan case. Batten reiterated that he knew nothing of Norfolk Savings's shaky health until just before the firm was shuttered. Huber again testified that he was unaware how its advertising was handled once it became insolvent.

On March 2, 1977, FCC Judge Kraushaar for the third time recommended that WTAR's license be renewed, opining that it would be impossible for media owners to investigate every piece of advertising copy to guarantee the honesty of an advertiser's management. And no guilt by association could be fastened to Batten, merely as a consequence of Huber's outside corporate business interests.

In 1975, however, the FCC had banned newspaper-television cross-ownership, meaning that a company couldn't own a daily newspaper and a TV or radio station in the same market. The U.S. Circuit Court of Appeals for Washington, D.C., in 1977 upheld the new rule. The court did not specifically order media companies with cross-ownership in seventy-nine cities, including Norfolk, to divest properties, but encouraged the FCC to do so. In June 1978, the U.S. Supreme Court backed the lower court.

Batten decided to sell WTAR. He issued a statement on March 31, 1979, expressing his frustration. "The contest has involved three exhaustive hearings, all of them resulting in strong rulings by an administrative law judge in favor of renewal of WTAR-TV's license. Still, there appears to have been no end to litigation which constitutes a heavy drain of management time and financial resources that would better be devoted to improvement of our newspapers, broadcasting stations and cable TV systems. Landmark believes . . . that FCC policy and these other obligations argue for settlement and divestiture," he explained in a news release.

Batten did not sell to Hampton Roads Television, however. Lustig and Campbell withdrew their application for the Channel 3 license in exchange for reimbursement of up to $750,000 of the expenses they'd incurred in the license challenge.

Batten spent about $50 million in lawyers' fees and watched the sheen wear on the reputation he so highly valued. "That's when I really started despising lawyers," he later said. He kept a quote from Shakespeare's play *Henry VI* on his desk: "The first thing we do, let's kill all the lawyers."

11 A Good Race

O NE OF BATTEN'S legacies from his Aunt Fay Slover was a love of sailing. She kept a yacht on Smith Creek, later renamed the Hague, a sliver of water near the Colonel's Norfolk home. Her first boat was a forty-foot cruiser, the *Mary Anne.* In about 1930, she traded up to the *Shadow J,* a fifty-five-footer bought for $35,000 from Miami Beach developer Carl G. Fisher.

George Purdy, whose family owned the Purdy Boat Company of Port Washington, New York, was captain of the *Shadow J* for the Slovers. In 1934, with the Depression in full swing, the Slovers commissioned Purdy Boat Company to build a sixty-foot replacement powered by four engines. The Purdys also crafted a twelve-foot knockabout sloop for young Frank and taught him to sail it.

When Fay Slover's new luxury yacht was completed, seven-year-old Frank Batten, wearing white shorts, dark blazer, and high-top dark leather shoes, stood on a wooden box to christen the *Shadow Fay.* The yacht cruised the St. Lawrence River's Thousand Islands for two summers, meandering along rivers and canals in New York and Quebec. Bound for home from one such excursion, Captain Purdy pulled the yacht into New York harbor so the Slovers could take in the World of Tomorrow, as envisioned by the 1939 World's Fair. Batten, aged twelve, saw the first public demonstration of the futuristic invention called television.

As a teenager, he sailed one summer at Culver Military Academy but over the years did little boating until he married. Jane had a dinghy and was the couple's avid sailor. They chartered a sailboat with friends Shirley and David Bradley for a week-long vacation on the Chesapeake Bay, and Frank was reinfected by the sailing bug.

Before long he ordered his own boat, a thirty-four-foot Tartan sloop with a pale blue hull. While that was being built in 1969, Batten sailed a loaner from the dealer, a twenty-seven-foot Tartan. Cruising quickly led to racing when a friend coached him on the finer points of competitive sailing. Jane went on a couple of races but preferred cruising—and had doubts about her husband's sailing abilities that were "well placed," Batten acknowledged. "I was a novice."[1] He won no points with his wife once he began competing in earnest: The races were always on weekends; he was rarely home.

Batten learned to sail competitively on the Tartan 34, which he christened *Shadow* after his aunt's boats. Already eyeing faster boats, the following year he moved up to a C&C Redline forty-one-footer named *Hallelujah* and had it shipped from Miami to Virginia on a tractor-trailer. After a single day's sail on the boat, renamed *Shadow II*, he signed up for a race in Hampton Roads. The *Shadow II* blew away the competition. For three years, Batten raced *Shadow II*, often crossing the finish line first. It was easy to spot the boat, which displayed a distinctive "7777" on the mainsail—numbers he kept for his next two boats. *Shadow II* took the second-place trophy in its class in the 1971 Annapolis to Newport race and in 1972 survived what may have been its most difficult race.

This was the 635-mile Newport Bermuda race, one of the toughest ocean races in the world, that year made tougher by the remnants of Hurricane Agnes. *Shadow* was one of 178 sailboats that departed Rhode Island's Narragansett Bay on June 16, 1972. It started with near perfect 20-to-23-knot winds and a forecast calling for moderate, southwesterly winds that would be supplanted by a cold front during the race. Once the front passed, light-to-moderate winds were expected to return to the race course.

It didn't happen. The front was stopped in its tracks when it smacked into Hurricane Agnes, by then downgraded to a tropical storm. A powerful tropical depression developed over the ocean between Florida and Bermuda, creating a dangerous spinning storm that hovered over Bermuda as the first boats approached the finish line.

Aboard the sailboats, the storm was "like driving a truck into a stone wall three times a minute for two days," *Yachting* magazine later reported.[2] Waves were so high that they broke over the yachts from bow to stern, stinging some deck hands so badly with saltwater that their eyelids were bruised and purple. With gale force winds up to 40 knots pummeling the yachts, some were forced to turn back.

Time and time again, *Shadow* climbed to the top of two- and three-story high waves, then fell into the watery trough below in a stomach-lurching roller-coaster ride. The wind howled through the rigging. Torrents of rain stung the helmsman like needles. On board *Shadow,* watch captain Jack Zanks had all he could do to stay on his feet when it was his turn at the wheel. Green water broke over the sloop and cascaded into the cabin, dumping saltwater directly onto the bunks. Batten was desperately seasick. Ray Brown, his navigator, was in such bad shape that he never left his berth, even though cold ocean water poured in on top of him. The crew tossed a piece of canvas over him to help keep him dry.

Morton Clark, a maritime lawyer, was the only one on Batten's boat who wasn't seasick. After finishing a four-hour watch, Clark went below and fixed himself Brunswick stew and topped it off with a banana, three brownies, and a martini. The skipper allowed the crew one drink a day when they were off watch. "Batten didn't say how big that drink had to be, though," he said, "so I was sitting there at the navigator's table and mixed myself a big gin on the rocks."[3] After dinner, he kicked back and prepared to light a stogie.

Batten tended to be soft-spoken, at least in public. It was a different story when competing in sailboat races, when he was known to let loose with ropes of expletives. "Everybody was throwing up and the son of a bitch was lighting up a cigar," said Batten. "If you light that cigar," he remembered telling Clark, "I'm going to throw your ass overboard."

Sailors were prohibited from using any electronic aids to navigate during the race. They relied on celestial navigation when they could get a sight and "dead reckoning," using only a compass, knot meter, and the clock to guide them to the finish line. With dense cloud cover and pelting rain, the crews could only guess at their position. On the fourth and worst day of the race, Eddie Wolcott, whom Batten admired as a great sailor, got off watch and told Batten in no uncertain terms, "This is the worst goddamn Monday night of my life."

Three Coast Guard cutters were dispatched to aid the endangered yachts. Three were dismasted and nearly every boat in the race was damaged, *Shadow* no exception. The Canadian-built sloop had slammed violently on its starboard side as it careened off a breaking wave. The noise was fearsome. One of the yacht's bulkheads, fiberglass partitions that separate the hull sections, shattered. Crew member Stan Brinkley remembered leaning against the bulkhead and feeling the damaged wall move every time *Shadow* rolled.

Shadow's exhausted crew sailed the last eighteen hours of the race on an ocean as flat as water in a bathtub. "After the blow came the calm," recalled Peter H. Willcox, whose forty-one-foot *Bones* was split apart after being slammed by a solid sheet of water.

Most boats limped into Bermuda in tatters. "We were the filthiest looking ragtag crowd I'd ever seen," Batten said. His crew hadn't shaved in five days and were still wearing the same soggy, vomit-caked clothes they'd embarked in. "We were in miserable shape. We just wanted to get ashore and get a drink." *Shadow* finished a respectable seventh out of thirty-five boats in its class.

Tom Hunnicut, who often sailed on *Shadow,* said Batten thrived on the planning stages of a race, giving each crew member a notebook with a set of detailed assignments. In the 1975 Annapolis to Newport Race, for example, Batten compiled twenty-six-page booklets with pre-race instructions, starting line directives, watch duties, and procedures for rescuing men overboard and abandoning ship. Such was its level of detail, said Hunnicut, that it helped foster teamwork.[4]

A good boat, like a good business, must thrive in whatever conditions are thrown at it. Business conditions change; boat designs change. Batten had several boats, but never budged on one racing feature: He refused to hire professional crewmen, even as the practice became common, and stuck with the crew he knew could excel.

It's a thinking man's game, said Stephen G. Kasnet of Boston, who crewed on the fifty-six-foot *Yankee Girl* in the '72 Newport Bermuda race. Success in both ocean racing and running a business requires hard work, good judgment, and a good crew.[5]

Donald H. Patterson Jr., a Landmark executive vice president whose forty-one-foot sailboat, *Orion,* in 2002 won the Onion Patch team racing series, said Batten took great pains in choosing the right people for the right job. "If there's any parallel" between ocean racing and business, Patterson said, "that's it. That is absolutely 100 percent what business is all about."[6]

And as in ocean racing, businesses don't always triumph immediately. "You keep working at it. Focus is extraordinarily important in racing and business. If you stay focused, just as in business, you succeed," Patterson said, and Batten had an instinct for both. Before making a big decision, Batten often solicited his crew's opinion. "He'd listen to everybody and then he'd make a decision and that was it, off we'd go," Clark said. "There was no second-guessing."

CNN founder Ted Turner, another avid sailor, was a bit of a Batten rival. The two were also friends, though their personal styles were diametrically opposed. Turner, nicknamed "The Mouth of the South," was boisterous and arrogant and in a race took no prisoners. Turner's bright red twelve-meter *American Eagle* set records from 1969 to 1974 in races around the world.

While the yacht was in a different class from Batten's *Shadow,* most of the boats in a race start together. Turner relied on speed and tactics over the course of a race to claim many a trophy; Batten relied on fast starts and often bested Turner off the line.

Apparently exasperated by Batten's ability to get a jump on him, Turner figured out a way to distract his media colleague. As one contest got under way, Turner's attractive French girlfriend took off her bikini top. Batten's crew forgot about the race, and the sails were left luffing.

"What's the matter with you bastards?" Batten shouted.

"Look over there, Frank," his crew cajoled.

Batten stared, too. *Shadow* lost time. "Turner beat us to death," Clark said.

In one race, however, Batten did beat Turner. "Of course, nobody had ever heard of us," recalled Conrad Hall, a *Shadow* crewman and Batten's longtime friend and colleague.[7]

"That will never happen again!" Turner shouted to Batten after their boats had tied up at the dock following the race. He swaggered down the pier to *Shadow*. "I've got to hand it to you," he told the winner. "I don't know how this crew of yours did it, but you all sailed a pretty good race and you should never have beaten me. The least I can do is take you down and show you a good crew and a good boat." Batten and the rest of *Shadow*'s crew followed Turner to his yacht, Batten carrying a drink in a small plastic cup.

Turner took great delight in showing off his state-of-the-art racer and offered drinks to his visitors. Stacked on a bar shelf were glass tumblers etched with "Turner Broadcasting." Turner poured the first drink for Batten and in a dramatic gesture held up the glass so the Turner company name faced Batten.

"Frank, see this?" he said. "I'm a big shot now."

Batten took his plastic cup, lifted it in the air as if he were making a toast, and turned it around so that Turner could see the name "Landmark Communications" printed on it. "I am, too," he said. His crew roared with laughter.

Billy Hunt, who also crewed aboard *Shadow,* said Batten was too nice to compete against some of the world's top ocean racers. "He enjoyed racing with his friends. There were no airs. He didn't need to impress or want to impress anyone. The others did."[8]

After the brutal 1972 Newport Bermuda race, Batten decided that he needed a bigger boat. Thumbing through *Yachting* magazine, he came across a photo of the year's hottest racing yacht, a black-hulled Swan forty-four-foot sloop created by Olin Stephens, designer of eight America's Cup winners. Batten asked that *Shadow* be painted on its stern, instead of *Shadow III.* "I didn't want to be advertising the fact that I was getting a boat every other year," he said.

The new *Shadow* came in second in its class in the 1973 Annapolis to Newport race and the 1974 Newport Bermuda race. With his next boat, a forty-six-foot Palmer Johnson sailboat bought from an Oxford, Maryland, boat dealer and built at the company's Wisconsin yard during the winter of 1975–76, Batten moved up a racing class. In the 1976 season the new *Shadow* won several races on the upper Chesapeake Bay, including the coveted Chesapeake Bay High Point Trophy. He took special pride that season in whipping *Running Tide,* "the winning-est boat on the Chesapeake Bay."

Batten's last Newport Bermuda race was in June 1978. Batten had donated his Palmer Johnson to the U.S. Naval Academy, and he and Clark were sailing on their pal Gene Sydnor's boat. Sydnor, who lived in Richmond, also had a forty-six-foot yacht, *Zephyr,* built by Palmer Johnson. Batten was watch captain and Clark was the navigator. They didn't win their class, but it was a good race. Seven months later, a car crash left Clark partially paralyzed. About the same time, Batten was diagnosed with the cancer that would cost him his vocal cords.

Batten knew there was virtually no chance that either one of them would ever sail competitively again. He told Clark: "When the skipper can't talk and the navigator can't walk, it's time to give up racing."

12 A Temporary Silence

URING THE WTAR license challenge, Batten had struggled with laryngitis-like symptoms that did not go away. A biopsy of his vocal cords in early 1977 revealed a cauliflower-like growth. Pathology reports came back negative. Batten was relieved. Over the summer, his voice improved. He had no time for sickness. The Norfolk Savings and WTAR debacles had consumed him, leaving precious little time to concentrate on Landmark or to attend to important duties as a member of the Associated Press board, to which he had been elected in 1975.

In October 1977, eight months after the final FCC hearing, Batten and other AP officers and directors set out on a journey to China. Their mission was to formally request that the AP open the first American news bureau in the country since 1949.

The AP, which bills itself as the world's oldest and largest newsgathering organization, in 1977 operated bureaus across the globe. The AP and Xinhua, the official Chinese news agency, regularly exchanged news and photos, but no official AP bureau had been established.

Today, the AP has three bureaus in China; in 2008, it brought in a team of 300 to cover the Olympics in Beijing.[1] China has become the world's second-largest economy, and according to one economist, will surpass the United States as the world's top economic superpower by 2027.[2] In 2010 it held more of America's foreign debt—$868 billion—than any other foreign country and had become the world's largest exporter.[3] China's Hong Kong–Shenzhen-Guangzhou region also had become the world's biggest "mega-region," home to 120 million people.[4]

But the China that the AP entourage found in 1977 was still internationally isolated and, to Batten, "remarkably obscure."[5]

Each of the Americans was assigned a numbered car and a driver. Kay Graham, publisher of the *Washington Post,* Arthur "Punch" Sulzberger, publisher of the *New York Times,* Stanton Cook, president of the *Chicago Tribune* and CEO of the Tribune Company, and Jack Tarver, chairman of the AP and vice chairman of Cox Enterprises, were among the guests who rode into town in the motorcade, their cars assuming place in line that reflected their office and seniority on the AP board. AP President Keith Fuller got a large black limousine. Everyone else had sedans made in Shanghai that resembled Plymouths from the late 1950s. The Battens' car, the color of pea soup, was no. 4.

The Americans were taken to the no-star high-rise Peking Hotel where they checked into poorly lighted, musty suites. The bathrooms were dirty, the rugs needed vacuuming, and the service was indifferent.

The country "stunned me," Batten wrote in the *Virginian-Pilot* when he returned to Norfolk. But after a couple of days, that which he had found alien and drab began to fade beside the country's natural beauty. The Americans visited the Great Wall and the Forbidden City in Beijing. They traveled by train to Mongolia and toured Shanghai. They went to hospitals, schools, and universities. They attended plays (among the acts in one play: "Renounce the Gang of Four," "The People Gloriously Carry Manure to the Fields," and "The Iron Man Finds Oil for the Motherland").

The highlight of the trip was the delegation's ninety-minute meeting with Vice Premier Deng Xiaoping in the Great Hall of the People located on the west side of Tiananmen Square in Beijing's city center. Home to the China National People's Conference, the Great Hall had 300 meeting rooms, an auditorium that seated 10,000, and a banquet hall where 5,000 diners could be served in one sitting.

The Americans and a delegation of Chinese officials were welcomed into a high-ceilinged room where they were directed to wicker chairs placed in a semicircle with spittoons between the chairs. An enormous oriental rug covered the floor; antique vases decorated tables.

Batten thought Deng, who stood shoulder-high to his six-foot frame, looked younger and stronger than his seventy-three years. Deng knew English but spoke through a translator. He delivered a droning monologue about education, workers' wages, the military, and a visit two weeks earlier by Cyrus Vance, President Carter's secretary of state. When the interpreter had difficulty translating a word into English, Deng helped him.

Batten was intrigued by Deng. Caught up in a political power struggle following the deaths of Mao and Premier Zhou Enlai, the vice premier had been sidelined by the leftist Gang of Four. Following their arrest for allegedly masterminding the Great Proletarian Cultural Revolution, Deng was brought back into the fold.

Smoking one cigarette after another, Deng was asked at the conclusion of the meeting why he had returned to office only two months before, given that the Gang of Four had been tossed out nearly a year earlier. "The creek isn't formed until the water arrives," Deng replied, drawing laughter from his Chinese comrades in the room. Batten walked out shaking his head.

Throughout the trip, Batten's voice became progressively strained and gravelly. He thought the incessant frog in his throat was from a cold. Or maybe he had been talking too much. One thing he was sure of: It wasn't from smoking cigarettes. He had dropped that habit in 1954 after shattering his leg on a ski slope in Stowe, Vermont.[6] While he still enjoyed an occasional Cuban cigar, he hadn't picked up a pack of cigarettes in nearly twenty-five years. But everyone in China smoked, the Chicago Tribune's Cook remembered, and Batten's voice "kept going down, down. We knew when we got back Frank was going to need some help."[7]

The country offered other challenges to respiratory health. Beijing was rapidly becoming almost uninhabitable because of smog produced by the soft coal used in homes and factories, and a gray haze hung over the city like soiled organza curtains. It coated the lungs with an "irritating concoction which produces wheezing, hacking coughs and endemic bronchitis," an AP bureau chief later wrote.[8]

By the end of the tour, Batten's throat was like sandpaper and he could barely talk. He went to see Dr. Gary Schechter, chairman of the Eastern Virginia Medical School's Department of Otolaryngology Head and Neck Surgery in Norfolk, who found new thickening of one vocal cord. Schechter referred him to Dr. Wilbur James Gould, a well-known New York ear, nose, and throat physician who had treated presidents, opera singers, and newscasters with voice problems.

In an examination, Gould found that Batten's polyps had recurred, but there was no visible sign of cancer. In December, Gould again scraped Batten's vocal cords. This time, Batten wasn't allowed to check out of the hospital. A biopsy revealed that the new growth was cancerous.

The six weeks of radiation treatments that followed tired Batten. He had always been on the go. When not at work, he was skiing, sailing, or playing tennis. Before his illness, longtime friend Colgate Darden would call Batten at work and tease his secretary, "Has Frank had his afternoon nap?" knowing that Batten was the least likely person to take a siesta. Once the daily treatments began, however, Batten found he did need to doze and stretched out on his office couch to rest.

Batten and his doctors were optimistic that the radiation therapy had obliterated the cancer cells, and over the next year his voice improved.

In the summer of 1979, after a routine biopsy, Batten was playing tennis with friends at the Norfolk Yacht and Country Club when he was summoned to the telephone. It was Gould. The cancer was back. Batten walked back to the tennis courts. He told his friends he had to leave. He didn't tell them why.

Gould recommended that Batten visit a specialist in Boston, one who was pioneering work with carbon dioxide lasers. Gould wasn't ready to recommend a laryngectomy, extreme surgery that would remove his entire larynx, or "voice box," if less radical laser surgery could knock out the cancer.

Batten flew to Boston to consult with Dr. M. Stuart Strong, who along with Dr. Gezo Jako had introduced the CO_2 laser to physicians who specialize in ear, nose, and throat disorders, successfully using laser on the larynx. Their first surgical laser was so large it was known as the "telephone booth."

Batten knew the laser surgery would compromise his ability to speak because part of his vocal cords would be removed. His voice would be raspy. He'd sound as if he was afflicted with a permanent case of laryngitis, but he'd still be able to talk, and it certainly would be far better than a laryngectomy.

Batten requested that the laser treatment be performed as quickly as possible. Frank Batten Jr., at the time a junior at Dartmouth College in Hanover, New Hampshire, drove to Boston to be by his father's side. The disease had forced Batten to face his own mortality. "Who will take over the company when I die?" he wondered.

From his hospital bed, he tried to persuade his only son to become a newspaperman—just as years earlier, his uncle had tried to convince him to join the family business. Feeling guilty that in his illness he was taking advantage of Frank Jr., Batten assured him he wouldn't be committing himself for life. "I was proposing that he come and see if he liked it."

Follow-up biopsies revealed that the laser surgery also had been unsuccessful—the only recourse now was to cut out Batten's vocal cords. In October 1979, nearly two years after his first diagnosis, Schechter performed a total laryngectomy, or opening in the windpipe. Batten was fifty-two. The surgery would have limited or ended most careers. Leaving the owner of a communications company with no natural ability to speak seemed doubly cruel.

Throughout the ordeal of treatments and surgery, Batten never lost his sense of humor, vouched Betty Moore, his secretary from 1967 to 1980. After the operation, hospital visitors thought they needed to speak loudly for Batten to understand them. Moore made a sign for "Mr. B," as she called him, that read, "I'M NOT DEAF. I JUST CAN'T TALK."[9]

He first used a hand-held electric larynx to communicate. Moore nicknamed Batten "R2D2," after the beeping and whistling mechanical droid from the movie *Star Wars*. In the weeks that followed, Batten mastered esophageal, or "belch" speech. Within a year, Schechter learned of a new technique for postlaryngectomy voice restoration that had been developed at Indiana University. Batten flew to Indianapolis to consult with physician Mark Singer and speech pathologist Eric Blom, who together had created an artificial voice box that enabled laryngectomees to speak in near-normal tones.

The Blom-Singer shunt operation involved creating a small hole in the wall between the windpipe and esophagus. A special one-way valve inserted into the opening allowed air from the lungs to be driven directly into the esophagus and prevented food from coming back into the trachea, Schechter explained.[10] This helped increase the volume of the voice from the esophagus.

Batten underwent surgery in Indianapolis to be fitted with the voice box, and in 1982 he was featured in a *Newsweek* magazine article about the new Blom-Singer artificial larynx.[11] Ties, ascots, or buttoned-up shirts hid the permanent tracheotomy. Over time, he was told he'd be able to speak in near-normal tones with regular voice inflections. In reality, there was nothing easy about the months of therapy ahead of him, and there were no guarantees that he'd ever regain his old vigor and command.

Batten's friends rallied for his struggle. In a letter sent to Batten about the time his cancerous vocal cords were removed, the *Washington Post*'s Kay Graham wrote on behalf of the "myriad of Batten fans to remind you of the deep affection—really love Frank—with which you are surrounded. I just hope you feel it and that in a small way, it helps."[12]

> I—and many others obviously—feel you are probably the best executive in our industry. At the risk of embarrassing you, let me say why: your company is run with emphasis on excellence of news, good *decent* forward looking management, growth of an inventive kind with a few well and rationally chosen acquisitions . . . your position in the industry is absolutely unique—

I know of no one who is so universally admired. On the other hand you didn't get there by trying to please but by deserving your reputation. All that said—you are not (a) goody two shoes—but funny & at times a little naughty about people & events around us.

His illness wouldn't compromise his talent for leadership, she told him. She'd back him and his "ambition, views, experience" over "someone else who can talk louder but has less to say."

13 Broadening Impact

BATTEN AS AP CHAIRMAN

I N THE SPRING of 1982, two and a half years after his cancer surgery, Batten was elected chairman of the 1,500-member Associated Press. Leading the AP, he said, motivated him to learn to speak again. The AP, for its part, pinned its hopes on his guidance.

Its finances were in bad shape. It had not kept up with changing technology. A discrimination lawsuit filed by seven of its female employees had not been settled after nearly a decade. As Batten saw it, the agency had little impetus to change: It had few competitors, was self-satisfied, and was resistant to change. The not-for-profit cooperative didn't have the capital to buy desperately needed new equipment. Its members were paying dues based on a formula nearly sixty years old and hopelessly obsolete.

AP directors volunteer their services to the cooperative while maintaining full-time jobs as publishers, presidents, or CEOs of their own news organizations. In 1975, after twenty years as a publisher himself, Batten had presented himself as a candidate for a seat on the AP board, whose directors are elected by the organization. When the ballots were counted, he had received more votes than any other candidate, including incumbents and the chairman. He would continue on the board for a dozen years, five as chairman.

Batten was passionate about the Associated Press. He had first learned of the news agency from Colonel Slover, who revered the AP and shared numerous stories illustrating its value with his nephew. Batten believed in its importance to the health of newspapers, particularly as they were increasingly challenged by television for customers. Though Batten was overwhelmed with health issues and kicking off the Weather Channel, as AP chairman he visited the

AP's Rockefeller Center headquarters in New York several times a month.

He'd ride the elevator to the seventh floor of "50 Rock," as the AP's offices were known to employees. Without fanfare, he wandered among the administrative offices. He chatted with newsroom reporters and editors on the fourth floor, asking questions and watching how people interacted with one another. He scanned office bulletin boards to get his own sense of the AP culture and stopped by the cafeteria for lunch.

By this time he had been fitted with his artificial voice box. As he practiced for his first board meeting as chairman—Batten was disdainful of the gender-neutral word "chair"—the AP's executive editor and vice president, Louis D. Boccardi, wondered whether he'd get through the session. He quickly found out. Batten ran meetings as though there wasn't a problem in the world with his voice, as if it were a minor annoyance he had to deal with, "when of course," Boccardi said, "it was a marvelous example of courage and valor."[1] After later delivering a ten-minute talk before hundreds of media executives at an American Newspaper Publishers Association conference, Batten said even he was surprised that he was not self-conscious about his gravelly voice.

In a letter to board members two months into his tenure, Batten reported that the AP's executives were smart, experienced, proud, dedicated, and highly motivated and "will give all they have to the AP."[2] He then listed four key opportunities to improve the organization, which he acknowledged were colored by his own views.

First, the AP's financial needs were more acute than the board recognized, and they were beginning to sap the organization's vitality and competitive strength. Communications and editing systems were falling behind the competition, particularly foreign news agencies like Reuters. There weren't sufficient cash reserves to maintain existing equipment. Start-up costs associated with opening new markets were out of reach.

Second, the AP traditionally served a stable, slow-to-change market. Faced with "turbulent change" in products and markets, the AP needed to seriously undertake long-range planning. Third, previous efforts to sell its news products had been "haphazard and lacking in continuity and creativity," Batten continued, and the news agency needed to market and promote itself more aggressively. Finally, compensation problems had to be addressed to deal with the "good many people" who were being paid below industry levels.[3]

Speaking at the Associated Press Managing Editors meeting in San Diego six months later, Batten revealed that the AP's debt was $13.1 million, more than quadruple its outstanding financial obligations reported eight years earlier. Not enough cash from its $173 million in revenues was being funneled into an equipment replacement account. Debt exceeded equity. Banks delivered a strong message to the AP that it had to finance more of its capital needs from internal funds rather than from loans.

There was a solution. The AP board, at Batten's urging, proposed a 9.5 percent increase in the assessment for its member newspapers; 6.4 percent for operations and 3.1 for a capital replacement fund. After studying ways to make the assessment structure equitable, in 1983 the AP board recommended fees that relied solely on newspaper circulation and level of service. It replaced an outdated, complicated formula using a member newspaper's targeted local population. Rates for some newspapers would go up under the new plan; others would drop.[4]

Batten and AP executives began knocking on publishers' doors to explain the business logic of a $9.5 million special assessment and the new rate system. The *Washington Post* was one of the newspapers in for a hefty rate hike, but the *Post* saw the wisdom of the assessment formula and accepted it, as did most of the other AP members.

With the new tariff plan in place, Batten asked Boccardi to write the first formal strategic plan that anyone could remember in the AP's 135-year history. He wanted to know where the AP had been, where it was now, what issues it faced, and what resources it needed to move forward. The organization needed to be smarter in managing its resources and wiser in planning its future instead of going from year to year on the momentum of a proud heritage.

It was "not some wreck of a business that didn't do anything right until Frank arrived," Boccardi pointed out. "We weren't at death's door, but we were not going to be able to grow and prosper and thrive running the place the old way."

During his tenure, Batten encouraged a more rigorous business environment, and with the change in the assessment formula the AP began heavily investing in additional new technology. Working with Kodak, the wire service participated in the invention of the digital camera. It became the first news agency to own a satellite transponder. It started a picture-a-minute digital photo service using computerized darkrooms and a high-speed delivery network for graphics.

Batten brought a disciplined approach to AP and at the same time believed it was a sin "not to try or not to venture." He was quietly demanding and had his own way of expressing his disappointment," recalled Boccardi. "He would say, 'It's not what I hoped for,' '(It's) not what I'm looking for,' 'This should be further along,' in a way that made you feel bad that you had somehow not fulfilled whatever it was he was asking you to do. That was part of the quiet strength that he had."

By the time Batten became AP chairman in 1982, the claims of discrimination by female members of AP had been mired in legal proceedings and were now part of a class action suit. Both sides were bitter. Enormous legal bills were piling up. The AP's decision-makers had refused to settle the case, preferring to take the fight to court. Katherine Graham, who had become the AP's first woman director in 1974, had urged the board to settle the suit for years in vain.

Batten pressed for a settlement. The AP ultimately paid more than $800,000 in back wages to women working at the news agency from 1972 to 1983. The seven women named in the suit shared $83,120.[5] Women made up 7 percent of the AP's staff when the suit was filed; the number rose to 22 percent when it was settled. As part of the consent decree, one-third of all new hires had to be women, 5 percent black and 5 percent Hispanic. Those goals were met and exceeded, said Batten.[6]

Batten's tenure as chairman was also marked by the 1985 kidnapping of AP chief Middle East correspondent Terry Anderson in Beirut, Lebanon, by a group of Hezbollah Shiite Muslims. During the six years and nine months that Anderson was held, AP executives arranged sensitive, off-the-record meetings with government officials, including retired Secretary of State Henry Kissinger and Oliver North, President Reagan's counterterrorism coordinator. Kissinger told the AP that the situation was discouraging and said there wasn't much they could do.

Whenever Batten and Boccardi met with AP employees in the United States or abroad, they were peppered with questions about what the AP was doing to free Anderson. "Frank agonized over the problem," said Boccardi. "He felt Terry's captivity was his responsibility as I felt it was mine."

Anderson, who was released on December 4, 1991, said he was grateful that Batten, Boccardi, and other AP executives did everything they could to gain his release. He was also thankful that the AP did not violate its ethics and integrity.[7] No deals or payoffs had been made.

While on the AP board, Batten traveled throughout the world visiting the news organization's bureaus and its major clients. During one trip to London when Batten was chairman, Queen Elizabeth II's daughter, Princess Anne, spoke at a black-tie dinner the AP hosted for British publishers in the paneled ballroom of the 1573 Middle Temple Court in London.

Batten congratulated Princess Anne for her courage after she had ripped into the British press, particularly singling out media baron Keith "Rupert" Murdoch, who owned, among other newspapers, the *Sun*, a British tabloid newspaper notorious for its topless "Page 3 girls."

Several months later, Murdoch and his wife visited Norfolk, Virginia, at the invitation of Jean Faircloth MacArthur, widow of

General Douglas MacArthur. She wanted Murdoch to tour the MacArthur Memorial, where her husband was buried and where the general's military archives were housed. Batten attended a luncheon in Murdoch's honor, hosted by Jean MacArthur. Still miffed by Princess Anne's diatribe, Murdoch snapped at Batten, "You're not much on picking speakers!"

At the annual meeting in May 1987, Batten gave his chairman's farewell speech to AP members, telling them that they had "cleaned out some cobwebs, altered some time-worn attitudes, and had become altogether a team more surefooted and serviceable."[8]

"It was not too long ago that AP had a reputation in some quarters for being smug, secretive, removed too far from the members it served," he concluded. "Happily that day is gone." The AP's financial position was "a strength rather than a problem." And the news agency no longer relied on "hand-to-mouth financing through ever-rising debt and assessment increases." He also reminded his audience that while there is always the temptation to become distracted by "exciting new media forms and technologies," there are no sounder businesses than newspapers and broadcasting. Boccardi, in his remarks, said Batten had asked the AP to be the best it could be and that Batten had led them to that high ground by his own example.

Batten was most pleased with having broken down the AP's culture of self-satisfaction and having helped to encourage the AP to change and improve while staying true to its essential mission.

In his final speech as chairman, he defined that mission in a passage later displayed at what was until 2004 the AP headquarters at 50 Rockefeller Plaza, on the lobby wall of the fourth-floor news operation: "The people of the AP are part of the fabric of freedom. They are the honest messengers, mostly anonymous, far from the limelight, often at risk and always committed to getting out the news as thoroughly and as accurately as possible."

"We all walked past it every day," said Dave Tomlin, the AP's associate general counsel, "but it still brings a lump to my throat."[9]

14 "A Preposterous Concept"

BATTEN HAD BEEN elected to head the AP in April 1982. One month later, the Weather Channel, his biggest—and riskiest—business venture was launched.

In the late 1970s, local newscasts offered weather forecasts for the following day. But weather segments were brief and easy to miss, nor did they offer the out-of-town forecasts that were important to business travelers. John Coleman, a weather personality on ABC's popular news-talk show, *Good Morning America,* believed that a national weather network, operating twenty-four hours a day, seven days a week, would serve a vital need. The big three broadcast networks, ABC, CBS, and NBC, weren't interested. A couple of newspaper companies saw potential in the concept but opted not to pursue it.

Frank Batten learned of Coleman's idea in April 1981. Landmark corporate staff member Bahns Stanley had been contacted by a Chicago-based venture capitalist who had worked up a business plan for Coleman, his poker buddy. Batten agreed to back Coleman, and plans for the Weather Channel were announced at a New York press conference in August. Batten and Coleman were in high spirits as they strode into the ballroom of the swanky Park Lane Hotel at Central Park South. Batten, learning to speak with the aid of a prosthesis, could barely contain his enthusiasm as he told reporters that this would be the first network devoted to news and information about the weather. Media representatives, most of them from trade journals, groaned. A press conference to be told that a channel was being planned for *weather?* They weren't the only skeptics. Industry insiders questioned why anyone would start a business venture that had folly written all over it.

Coleman was named the Weather Channel Inc.'s chairman, president, and chief executive officer as part of his July 1981 management and consulting agreement with Landmark. He held 20 percent of the new network's voting stock; Landmark had the rest and supplied all of the capital. Coleman oversaw the network's day-to-day operations, but according to his contract, if the network didn't meet mutually agreed-upon financial targets, he would be out and Landmark would take control.

The Weather Channel's first home was in a nondescript building in an office park in Vinings, a pleasant Atlanta suburb. The southern hub was chosen because it boasted satellite up-link capability for both Coleman's segments on *Good Morning America* and for the Weather Channel.

The early days were anything but smooth. The bugs were being worked out of new technology. Finding advertisers was a challenge. An all-weather network was such uncharted territory that live broadcasts had more than their share of missteps.

Early advertising campaigns and on-air promotions were created on a shoestring. Kathy Lane, who later became vice president for public relations, recalled rounding up Annie, her golden retriever, to star in "Weather and Your Pet" features. Lane's son was filmed in a shoe store for a back-to-school segment. If an ad for masonry paint was to be filmed, Lane asked if anyone needed their garage painted. Weather maps were all hand-drawn on art cards.[1]

Some of the best meteorologists in the country had been hired, including Ken May Jr. from the Strategic Air Command's weather station in Omaha, Nebraska; Mark Mancuso, TV weatherman in Knoxville, Tennessee; Ray Ban, working at AccuWeather in State College, Pennsylvania; Bill Keneely with WTVT in Tampa, Florida; and Dennis Smith from what today is KSNW-TV in Wichita, Kansas. Initially there was little furniture or equipment at the fledgling network's office. Mancuso remembered coming to work and sitting on folding chairs.

Those early days were an exciting time to be immersed in what the network's pioneers loved best: weather. They were young, optimistic, and playful, but not always professional. On air, the Pocono Mountains became the "Pinocchio" Mountains. The La Jolla Sorghum Festival was announced as the California city's "Scrotum" Festival. Butte, Montana, became "Butt" Montana. The OCMs, short for on-camera meteorologists, played practical jokes on each other while on the air, from tossing lighted matches to intentionally airing footage of gorillas instead of mountain ranges.

Coleman did not share his staff's high spirits. As far as he was concerned, the new recruits were trying to undermine him. In his deep voice he would say, "Young man . . . I'm not amused."

The Weather Channel's first live shot was of a solar eclipse on May 30, 1984. That evening, a technician lugged a telescope to the roof of the suburban Atlanta studios and aimed a camera in the direction of the coming celestial event. At the appointed moment, viewers were treated to footage of the first stage of the eclipse. By the time the broadcast cut back to the roof, the camera angle had changed. Viewers saw another orb in the sky—a circular orange gas station sign, blocks away. "Look, there's a Gulf station on the moon!" weather forecaster Al Lipson exclaimed.[2] During another live broadcast, two window washers unwittingly began scrubbing the forecast center panes behind meteorologists Bruce Edwards and Jim Cantore.

The new cable television network also provoked skepticism among industry insiders. It was an easy target for jokes. David Letterman jested that it was "reassuring to know that you can wake up at 4 o'clock in the morning and find out the relative humidity in Manila."[3] Meanwhile, advertisers stayed away. Batten owned a cable company himself and believed cable industry experts who predicted that cable advertising billings would soar from $45 million in 1980 to $2.2 billion by 1990.[4] In fact, the most attractive advertiser-supported cable networks, including ESPN and CNN, had built up an advertising base and were so popular among viewers that cable operators paid *them* a monthly carriage fee to remain on their cable systems. But the Weather Channel was too new, too untried, too quirky to lure many advertisers. And it certainly could not demand carriage fees.

By 1983, the Weather Channel was experiencing tremendous operating losses. Landmark, which had anticipated losses of $924,000 during the first year, instead found its coffers depleted by more than $15 million.[5] The company was continuing to write checks for $840,000 a month to stay on the air. Employees found Coleman's behavior explosive and erratic.

Months earlier, Coleman appealed for help from Dubby Wynne, at the time head of Landmark's Broadcasting and Video Enterprises division. Wynne temporarily turned over his Norfolk duties to Landmark president Dick Barry and took charge of the Weather Channel's advertising sales, marketing, and business administration to try to get the network's finances back on an even keel. A personnel consultant, hired by Landmark to measure morale of the network's employees, reported back that the survey results were the worst he had seen in thirty years.

According to Coleman's contract with Landmark, if the Weather Channel did not reach 87.5 percent of its targeted operating income in its first year, he could be fired. The year was nearly up. The Weather Channel's balance sheet was wretched. Batten wanted Coleman out of day-to-day management. In April 1983, Batten asked Coleman to stay on as chairman but said he would have to step down as president and CEO. Batten offered Coleman a raise to be the network's spokesman and said he would still play a role as a program consultant. In Coleman's place, Batten would hire a seasoned executive who had a better chance at turning the network around.[6] Wynne followed up the proposal in writing.

Coleman refused to budge. On June 27, 1983, Coleman went to a Georgia Superior Court to ask for a temporary restraining order to block his ouster from the Weather Channel.

In a hearing the following day, Coleman's attorney told the judge that if Coleman was squeezed out his client would be "irreparably harmed." Landmark's attorney claimed that the Weather Channel was "hopelessly insolvent," citing the network's enormous deficit during its first year of operation. Coleman didn't dispute the fact that there were cost overruns but said the expenditures had been forced on him by Landmark. On the witness stand, Batten contradicted Coleman, calling the contention that Landmark was responsible for cost overruns "an utter fabrication. On no occasion did I ever tell Coleman to increase expenditures."

Most of the Weather Channel staff had heard that the network was in financial trouble, but the extent of its problems was not common knowledge. Several employees showed up for the hearing. Meteorologist Bill Matley said it was like being at a wedding; employees from the Weather Channel were on one side of the aisle; Landmark executives were on the other. Matley understood the reality of business: Coleman was a bad manager. Even so, he sat on Coleman's side of the room. "It was kinda sad. I felt bad for Coleman, letting his pride get in the way."[7]

The following day, the judge ruled in Coleman's favor.[8] With the order preventing him from being fired, Coleman had control of the business. "John Coleman had gone into the lion's den and almost bearded the lion," recalled Barry, later named Landmark's vice chairman. "This guy, with no money, had pushed us into a corner. There was no graceful way out."[9]

In the end, Batten had no choice but to shut down the Weather Channel. He didn't sleep a wink the night before reporting his decision to the Landmark board of directors. Years later he recalled the board meeting was like a wake. Some of the directors thought the whole idea of a weather network had been crazy to begin with, but they hadn't second-guessed him, at least not to his face.

Louis Ryan, Landmark's corporate counsel, calculated that the best way to get rid of Coleman was to "cut off the money, period, and let the thing rot." But he knew that was not the Landmark way. "Frank was a leading advocate for saying, 'We've got an awful lot of employees down there and we have to treat them right,'" Ryan said. "We also had a reputation in the communications industry and to just go dark one day is not the Landmark way, either."[10] Batten and Wynne hoped Coleman would be cooperative so the Weather Channel could close down in an orderly manner. They would abide by their contracts with cable affiliates and give them ninety days' notice that the network was folding.

On July 8, 1983, Batten made it official. He dictated a letter to Phillip E. Couri, Coleman's Winnetka, Illinois, lawyer and a Weather Channel board member. "Accordingly," it read, "you are advised that effective immediately, Landmark has discontinued funding of the Weather Channel."

There was enough money to meet payroll for the work week ending July 16. Landmark would continue paying the bills for ninety days only if the Weather Channel's board of directors—Batten, Wynne, Coleman, and Couri—agreed to a program of orderly liquidation at a meeting to be held in Atlanta. "The Weather Channel," the letter concluded, "is insolvent."

Batten called a meeting of the network's board for July 11 in the twenty-fifth-floor offices of King & Spalding, Landmark's downtown Atlanta attorneys. Coleman asked for a delay. They met four days later and on that hot Friday afternoon, the board members took their seats. There was no small talk. The atmosphere was cordial but tense. Batten got down to business. If Coleman was going to run the network into the ground with Landmark's money, Landmark was going to turn off the tap and stop the flow of cash.

"For some reason, it had not dawned on him that we would do that," Barry said. "He probably just assumed, somewhat naively, that we would just continue to write checks."

Despite the court order, which had frustrated and angered Batten, he wanted a businesslike resolution. He was a gentleman, not a corporate buccaneer, and it was his duty to make a good-faith effort to come to terms with Coleman. He also was well aware that the likelihood of that happening was slim. Coleman had assumed Batten was bluffing about closing the Weather Channel. Faced with the finality and stark terms of Batten's resolution, he was stunned.

That afternoon the board voted to dissolve the Weather Channel. Coleman finally knew they were serious. Batten was not inclined to win at all costs. "It wasn't like pulling one of these deals like they do in the textile industry where they just announce to everybody, 'By the way, you're fired,'" Ryan said. "That is not something Frank Batten would ever do."

Conrad Shumadine, an attorney with Willcox Savage,[11] Landmark's outside legal counsel in Norfolk, was the only one at the board meeting not directly affiliated with the weather network. He met privately with Coleman during a two-hour recess and urged him to accept Batten's offer: Stay on at the Weather Channel and let someone else with business acumen run it. Landmark would continue to pay him, and he could retain his stock. Shumadine got nowhere.

When the meeting resumed, Coleman announced that he wanted to buy the Weather Channel. He asked Batten for sixty days to find a backer. Batten agreed to thirty days. Coleman would have to come up with $4 million for the network's assets, plus $15 million for the satellite transponder and up to a million dollars to cover the operating deficit during the thirty days. Even Coleman's lawyer thought the veteran weatherman was being foolhardy. "I don't think it's near enough time," Couri cautioned his client.

"I assure you, it is," Coleman shot back.

"John, nothing's going to happen in thirty days," Couri insisted.[12]

The meeting adjourned with details to be ironed out the next day. Batten put Dick Barry in charge and told his senior executives to work it out with Coleman or to scratch the deal. Batten flew home to Norfolk. "A lot of business people would have felt this was a confrontation between them and John Coleman and would have wanted to be there for the surrender," said Tommy Johnson, a Willcox Savage attorney.[13]

Lawyers met Saturday morning and pushed for closure by the afternoon. The air conditioning was on a timer and had powered down for the weekend. Suit jackets and ties came off. Shirtsleeves were rolled up. Coleman's Atlanta attorney was getting agitated. The process, he complained, was taking too long. By about 5 p.m., still with no final agreement in hand, he announced that his wife had planned a dinner party and he was leaving.

Barry had been waiting for a moment like this. "You can go home if you want to," he told the lawyer. "But let me tell you the consequences of our not getting this deal done. Unless we work out a deal this weekend, we are going to pull the plug on the Weather Channel on Monday morning. The entire staff will be notified that they cannot come to work anymore if they expect to get paid."

He turned and addressed Coleman. "If you go to work and deceive the employees about the availability of funds, that's a crime in the state of Georgia." He handed him a copy of the statute. Coleman and his lawyers were surprised by the threat. The Virginia gentlemen were getting tough.

Couri told his colleague to go home. Couri and the Landmark lawyers began to crank out drafts of a settlement agreement. Willcox Savage attorney Rebecca Beach Smith, now a U.S. District Court judge for the Eastern District of Virginia, researched legal questions in the King & Spalding library throughout the night as colleagues plied her with coffee and doughnuts. Wynne, who had worked the closest with Coleman and drew the greatest wrath from the volatile weatherman, stayed in the background. Ryan, with his infectious laugh and penchant for easing strained bargaining sessions, wisecracked and kept the group going. Barry stayed in contact with Batten by telephone. Coleman drank gallons of Tab and napped on a sofa in the firm's foyer.

Early Sunday morning, an agreement was reached. Coleman had thirty days to buy the network or all ownership and control reverted to Landmark. Coleman remained chairman and CEO, but Landmark was fully in charge of the Weather Channel's finances. Coleman agreed to drop his earlier lawsuit. Ryan pulled a twenty-dollar bill out of his wallet and handed it to Coleman, buying back the weather forecaster's 20 percent interest in the network. Landmark's negotiators, "all depressed as hell," got on a plane and returned to Virginia.[14] Coleman was upbeat and smiling. He left the marathon meeting and immediately started making calls to potential backers.

Everyone had made fun of a 24-hour weather network and now

it was going under. "It was very disconcerting," for Batten, Smith recalled. "His pride was on the line."[15]

One New York media analyst, who called the Weather Channel "one of the most preposterous concepts" on cable television, predicted that the only hope of keeping the business off the cable scrap heap would be through a merger.[16] The Weather Channel was nearly dead.

As Wynne was preparing the company's liquidation, a cable operator telephoned. The weather network was popular among viewers, he told Wynne, and if it meant keeping it on the air, he'd consider paying Landmark subscriber, or carriage, fees. Wynne told the cable operator that he was prohibited from talking to him during Coleman's option period, but a seed had been planted.

He and Batten were stunned by the suggestion. Only a few cable programmers were paid fees. Most cable operators received nothing to supply programming. In fact, as more programming options became available, some new networks paid the cable companies.

Batten and his team began to wonder: With Coleman out of the picture, could they save the Weather Channel? While they could do nothing for thirty days, rumors were flying throughout the industry that Coleman was having no luck finding anyone with deep pockets.

Coleman unsuccessfully approached forty-six possible sources of financing for the necessary $4 million down payment, including Ted Turner.[17] After a luncheon meeting with two of Turner's vice presidents, Coleman was told Turner had no interest in shoring up a struggling weather network. He had enough of his own problems pushing back stiff competition from CNN, his three-year-old news operation.

On August 15, with his option about to expire, Coleman issued a twelve-sentence statement to his staff. Underlined were the words "Goodbye . . . Thank you . . . Good luck . . . So long."

Wynne, who was now spending most of his time at the Weather Channel, met with each of the 160 staff members and asked them for input. "What's good?" he wanted to know. "What's bad? What do we need to change?"

Batten flew to Atlanta to personally thank workers for their dedication. He didn't sugarcoat the Weather Channel's challenges but told them he and Wynne would do everything they could to keep the network on the air. Landmark set a three-month deadline to gauge the willingness of cable operators to pay carriage fees and to develop a strategy. If 80 percent of the Weather Channel's subscriber base agreed to the fee plan, they decided, Landmark would keep the network on the air.

The Weather Channel got commitments from up to 70 percent of cable operators. Over the next several years, both cable fees and distribution were forthcoming from almost all the cable companies. The Weather Channel was on its way to solvency.

15 The Weather Channel Takes Off

T HAT THE Weather Channel made it beyond those first couple of years "was a damn miracle, frankly," Dubby Wynne, CEO, confided.[1] Within the three-month time frame Landmark had established after Coleman left the network, Wynne set up appointments with the top brass at each cable company, who alone would authorize the fee plan. CNN was charging cable operators about fifteen cents each month per subscriber. USA Network's monthly fee was around ten cents per subscriber. The Weather Channel could break even in about three years with just a nickel a customer. While big entertainment companies would have "thrown their baby out the window" before they'd reveal their balance sheets, Wynne said, the Weather Channel opened its books. Here's what we expect to charge, he and the company's other pitchmen told operators. Here's what we expect to achieve if we do.

He credited the reputation of TeleCable and its executives, Dick Roberts and Gordon Herring, as among the key reasons why so many cable operators were willing to support the Weather Channel. "If they had not paid us those fees," he said, "we would not have continued the service, period." At the network's launch, Landmark had "no market leverage at all. Zero," Wynne said. "We were lucky with timing but we put together a decent business plan and we were honest with them and they supported us." Other cable programming companies weren't so lucky, and many start-ups folded.

Innovative technology played a key role. At its launch, the Weather Channel had planned to provide regional, but not local weather forecasts every half hour. Alan Galumbeck, working on the Landmark corporate staff, came up with the concept of Weather STAR—Satellite Transponder Addressable Receiver—a technology that provides around-the-clock local weather forecasts—the

"Local on the 8s"—as well as local advertising crawls at the bottom of the local forecasts, local severe weather advisories, and enhanced radar maps. TV stations nationally copied it with their own variations of the Weather Channel's "Local on the 8s."

The Weather STAR is a device located at each cable system that receives a stream of weather data sent via satellite along with the audio and video from the Weather Channel. The STAR selects the data that apply to its local community, creates a visual representation of those data, and imposes that visual onto the Weather Channel video. Over the years, there were at least five major versions of STAR technology, improving computing and graphic capabilities. A new STAR capable of supporting the Weather Channel's transition to high definition format was the newest generation, built as part of the Weather Channel's $50 million transition from standard definition to HD television. State-of-the art studios and new broadcasting equipment using HD-TV technology also were included.

Landmark also invested millions of dollars in the Weather Channel's feature programming, such as the hour-long *Storm Stories*. The longer evening shows usurped the popular "Local on the 8s," although local weather conditions were still available at the bottom of the screen. Ratings went up. The Weather Channel still strove to please its long-time loyalists, of course, but the new features appealed to a new generation of viewers.

The Weather Channel grew from "a man and a map" to the most respected weather news and weather programming network in the country, producing all its weather forecasts from its own global forecast center and employing more than 100 meteorologists to interpret the data, then produce and deliver forecasts. It also passed on to affected localities tornado, hurricane, and other severe weather watches and warnings issued by the government's meteorologists. National and local broadcast and cable TV meteorologists imitated the Weather Channel and began to cover weather live—even giving forecasts while clinging to signposts to keep from being blown away by high winds and pounding rain.

The Weather Channel's on-air meteorologists were celebrities.

Paul Goodloe was picked for a *People Weekly* magazine's "Beautiful People" issue. Jim Cantore likely is the most well-known weatherman, the one many cable TV viewers expect to see on air when a bad storm approaches. Alexandra Steele made a cameo appearance in a season finale of the *Friends* TV show. Heather Tesch is "our gorgeous lady" according to one website. Most weren't as young as Stephanie Abrams when she was hired in 2003 at the age of twenty-three. Abrams was only three years old when Batten began the network. Jeff Morrow reassured more than one person on a trip to Hatteras Island on the Outer Banks of North Carolina that he was there to visit his parents, not because a major storm was on the way. Tropical weather expert Steve Lyons has autographed tennis shoes and body parts. Even Robert Simpson, former director of the National Hurricane Center and cocreator of the Saffir-Simpson Scale used to gauge hurricane strength, was a fan of the Weather Channel. It is, he said, "absolutely unique." In 2009, the ninety-six-year-old Simpson said that while confined to a wheelchair, he checked out weather .com for his local Washington, D.C., weather and weather maps.[2]

One of the Weather Channel's most important innovations was the creation of the website, named "weather.com," launched in 1995. Batten and Wynne had sensed that they would have to compete against their own products to survive in a medium that was evolving toward an Internet-centric business model. After making minimal investments during the site's first two years, when weather.com was bringing in only a couple of million dollars in revenue and no profit, Landmark increased its commitment in 1997. Weather.com would chalk up $50 million more in losses from 1997 until 2003, when it would break even and begin to make a profit.[3]

Even by 2000, however, when the website was generating only around $20 million in revenue, two major investment bankers were suggesting valuations as high as $2 billion for weather.com.[4] The site was then delivering weather-related information to more than 77,000 cities and towns worldwide and attracting nearly fifteen million visitors monthly. Although Batten could have made short-term gains as measured by the stock market if he had taken weather.com public, he believed an initial public stock offering would have been incompatible with Landmark's goal of creating long-term growth in value. Batten wondered what would be left for the next generation of weather.com employees if the value of the company was handed out early on.

According to Debora J. Wilson, the network's president until February 2009, during the Internet heyday those offered stock options during a company's IPO made the most money when the shares that had been purchased for pennies often were sold for hundreds of dollars more per share in a matter of months. Employees who joined a company later received options at market price, so their opportunity to make money was completely dependent on the stock market. If the stock price went up, they would benefit, but to a much lesser degree than pre-IPO employees. If the stock market went down, "their shares were under water."

Landmark didn't need the capital to grow the business. Batten, no doubt remembering the Weather Channel's fragile beginnings and his tussle with Coleman, did not want to lose operating control. Further, he didn't think it was fair for one small group of employees to be offered stock options when everyone else at the Weather Channel and Landmark was working equally hard and did not have the same privileges.

In March 2000, Landmark paid $120 million in cash for Weather Services International, a sister to the Weather Channel providing weather products to more than 5,500 clients in forty-five countries serving the media, aviation and utility companies, and government sectors. With offices in the Boston area and in Birmingham, England, WSI was the first private weather company to provide real-time weather data, graphic production systems, and custom weather shows to the Weather Channel, as well as to half of the country's local broadcast stations and to satellite and cable services.

It was the first to offer international satellite imagery to the marketplace, and the first to develop a professional systems-level product to track hurricanes and typhoons. With its WSI Pilotbrief and WSI InFlight, the company also produced weather data and meteorological systems to aviation clients including 80 percent of all commercial airlines and cargo carriers as well as the Federal Aviation Administration's command center.

Other efforts at international expansion had been less successful. In June 1996, Landmark launched its first European weather network. At its peak, there were an estimated twenty million viewers via the Weather Channel U.K., broadcasting through Great Britain and Ireland; Het Weer Kanaal, a Dutch language network transmitted from London, which served the Netherlands, Belgium, Luxembourg, and other parts of Europe; La Chaine Meteo in France; and Il Canale Meteo in Italy. It owned a 45 percent interest in Der Wetter Kanal, with viewers in Germany, Austria, German-speaking Switzerland, and the Czech Republic.

But Landmark had failed to recognize that foreign cable markets, as well as consumers' viewing habits, were radically different from those in the United States. The European cable market was fragmented by too many languages. The advertising market was puny. Days before the Weather Channel's English counterpart went on the air, Pelmorex, the U.S. operation's Canadian rival, launched its own UK channel called the Weather Network. There were complexities in dealing with foreign governments and companies to secure needed weather data systems. Because cable wasn't as big in Europe as it was in America, the viewing audience was smaller.

Britain is smaller and its weather is not nearly as varied as in the United States, British media pointed out, nor does the UK share the same zealous interest in weather. The British magazine the *Tatler* summed it up: "The U.S. is a vast country, prone to hurricanes, earthquakes, showers of frogs and plagues of locust, so viewers in the more temperate regions can enjoy a shiver of relief at the meteorological misfortunes of their fellow countrymen. Over here, our weather is like our politics: reliably dull across the whole country." A cable industry trade magazine offered several more reasons for the failure of the Weather Channel's overseas effort: "Poor distribution, paltry or non-existent license fees, cultural-protection laws and labor issues."

Nevertheless, the Weather Channel and Pelmorex fought for British viewers. Landmark won a major victory on the satellite front when it signed a distribution agreement with Rupert Murdoch's BSkyB. That left the lucrative cable market up for grabs until a subsidiary of Telecommunications Inc. announced it would acquire half of Pelmorex. Since TCI already owned 50 percent of the UK cable market, that was bad news for Batten. He shifted gears. In September 1996, Landmark signed a deal for part ownership of Pelmorex's Canadian weather networks.

When it closed in December 1997, Landmark's Weather Channel Europe had amassed the largest losses of Batten's career. The Weather Channel Europe was a "real dog," Batten said.[5] He had failed to trust his instincts and ignored warning signs. The networks not only should have been closed sooner, he said, but they never should have been created to begin with.

Batten, in his book about the Weather Channel, summed up the European defeat:

> Unfortunately, all the projections were based on a pyramid of assumptions, which is the shakiest kind of pyramid. If any of the fundamental assumptions are wrong, then every subsequent calculation has to be wrong. And when you stack a second bad assumption on top of that first one, things can go way wrong. As it happened, we misfired on most of our assumptions: distribution, full-time versus part-time carriage, pricing, audience, and advertising. The projections were more or less the mathematical sum of everything we wanted to have happen. Instead of earning attractive returns, we found out, we were soon incurring huge losses.[6]

Batten had similar failures in Latin America. In the fall of 1996, Landmark began broadcasting El Canal del Tiempo, serving Spanish-speaking Latin America and the Caribbean. O Canal do Tempo provided forecasts in Portuguese. The meteorology reports, originating from the Weather Channel studios in Atlanta, were the first such programming on the South American continent.

By 1999, El Canal del Tiempo could be seen in fourteen Latin American countries. In 2001, the combined networks had ten million subscribers. The network's challenges were overwhelming, however. Meteorologists serving Latin America wrestled with how to present forecasts for two hemispheres, varying seasons, multiple languages, and numerous dialects. Even national boundaries created problems. At one point, a border treaty between Argentina and Chile made the network's map obsolete. More problematically, no central source provided weather data for Latin America; it might come from the government, the military, or private companies. Some areas lacked overnight weather updates because reporting stations closed at 9:30 p.m.

Citing plummeting economies and fragile political structures, and after pouring $40 million into the Latin American start-ups over six years, Landmark disbanded El Canal del Tiempo and O Canal do Tempo in 2002.

While the Weather Channel's television programming was its mainstay, in later years its greatest growth in revenue would come from the Weather Channel Interactive, Inc., which included weather.com, broadband, wireless, desktop, and subscription services. Cell phones would be able to receive live radar and weather reports, while Notify!, a subscription weather alert service, could warn of a nearby tornado. By the time the Weather Channel was sold in the autumn of 2008, weather.com would have websites specifically for the United Kingdom, France, Latin America, and Brazil. Posting current weather conditions, forecasts, and lifestyle content for 100,000 locations around the globe, it would reach close to forty million unique users each month.

Batten conceded that while he made mistakes in business, he didn't spend his life trying to avoid making them. His philosophy: Make the assumption you're going to win and don't commit suicide if you fail. Some people go through life in a defensive mode to protect themselves against failure, which is something he never did. He thought it was a waste of time.

16 Landmark Continues to Grow

A
FTER THE DECADE of FCC challenges to Landmark's
ownership of Norfolk's WTAR-TV, in August of 1980 Batten agreed to sell the Norfolk station to Knight-Ridder
Newspapers, Inc. The following January, the FCC approved the
sale for $48.3 million, and the station changed hands that March.
Greensboro station WFMY-TV had already been sold in 1976. Batten had not lost interest in ownership of television stations, however.
Broadcast holdings would be one of the areas of Landmark's diver-
sification during the 1980s and 1990s.

Landmark had long owned two Norfolk radio stations. WTAR-
AM in Norfolk had been the first radio station in Virginia, broad-
casting in September 1923 over a 15-watt transmitter that could be
heard for ten miles. The *Ledger-Dispatch* acquired the station in
October 1932 for $15,000. WTAR-FM went on the air in 1947, and
fifteen years later its call letters had been changed to WLTY, "We
Listen to You." Landmark would sell both stations to Benchmark
Communications of Baltimore in 1993 for $4.5 million.

At various times Landmark owned several television stations. It
acquired KNTV in San Jose, California, in December 1977 for $24.5
million and sold it to Granite Broadcasting Corporation in 1990 for
$59 million. On July 1, 1978, Landmark bought KLAS-TV for $9.6
million from the estate of Howard Hughes, who had died in 1976.
The Las Vegas, Nevada, station had been a poor performer for the
Hughes organization but would prove a bargain in a city that later
exploded in population.

Included in the KLAS deal was a former motel with an associated
one-story green cinderblock bungalow at 336 Cathedral Way that
the eccentric Hughes had bought in 1953. Insomniac and morbidly
afraid of germs, Hughes had ordered the casement windows in the

bungalow sealed and installed airlocks on the doors. When he left in 1954, an air conditioner and air recycler were installed at the back of the house to keep the air pure. He left his clothes and other belongings inside with an order that they were not to be touched.

He'd watch movies in the middle of the night, and as an added benefit in those pre-VCR days, if Hughes fell asleep during the film, he'd have an aide telephone the station and demand that the movie be rewound and restarted where he dozed off. The operator on duty complied.

Long-time KLAS-TV executive Bob Stoldal remembers anchoring the 11 p.m. newscast when Hughes was in town. He'd often have an aide call Stoldal after the newscast. "Mr. Hughes was watching the news and wants more information on the United States Nuclear Test Ban treaty. Please record the information and a security guard will pick it up."

"That was the routine," Stoldal recalled. "I would dig up whatever I could, record it, the security guard would pick the machine up. The next day when I got back to work the machine was back on my desk. It was one of those old big reel-to-reel machines. A couple of times I heard Hughes's voice in the background yelling at the aide: "Tell him I want that now; make him understand."[1]

Hughes died in 1976. As part of the 1978 agreement to buy the station, no one from Landmark could enter the "Hughes home" unaccompanied by a Hughes agent for one year because of the possibility that Hughes's missing will might be hidden in the cottage. Representatives of the estate looked behind walls, removed bricks in the fireplace, and ripped up flooring, but found nothing. When the house was reopened, remembered station employee Joan Carlton, there were unopened cereal boxes in the cupboards, a jar of mustard on the kitchen counter, and Hughes's soap in the two bathrooms. Landmark renovated the home and used it as an overnight guest house for meetings and to entertain clients.

Eventually, it became a Howard Hughes museum of sorts, said Dick Fraim, the station's general manager, who retired in 2004. KLAS-TV employees took delight in showing visitors Hughes's office desk and chair, reel-to-reel tape deck, and Edison Voicewriter dictating machine. On the walls were an architect's rendering of a hangar proposed for the Hughes Air Terminal in Las Vegas, a photo of the New York ticker tape parade that greeted Hughes when he returned from breaking the around-the-world air speed record in 1938, and a nearly life-sized photo of Hughes at the editing table during the filming of his movie *The Outlaw*, starring Jane Russell.

Nashville's WTVF-TV was bought by Landmark in 1992 for $43.5 million. At a time when most of the nation's broadcast stations were run by white men, Lemuel E. Lewis, KLAS-TV's general manager and an African American, was tapped by Landmark as Nashville's president.

Lewis, a graduate of the University of Virginia, where he also earned an MBA, followed a station manager who'd been an extremely well-liked community leader. Batten took a tremendous risk by sending him to Nashville, Lewis figured. Businesses might have withdrawn their advertising dollars in protest. They did not, perhaps because Lewis wasn't out to shake things up. Rather, he cut expenses and increased profitability while retaining the station's status as the most-watched in town, and returned to the corporate staff in 2000, becoming Landmark's chief financial officer.

The CBS affiliate, where Oprah Winfrey got her start in the business in 1974, began calling itself NewsChannel 5 Network in 1999 to reflect its growing family of products, including online, radio, and NewsChannel 5+, a news and information cable channel. *Talk of the Town*, its midday talk and entertainment show, was the longest-running locally produced talk show in the country. NewsChannel 5 also excelled in investigative reporting, winning broadcasting's highest honors, the Peabody and Columbia-duPont awards.

In a speech in 1984, Batten told Landmark's senior managers that to maintain the public's trust, investigative reporting must have a clear and important purpose and should be directed and edited with care and meticulous attention to accuracy and fairness.[2] The station's "Friends in High Places" series by reporter Phil Williams was just such reporting. It rocked the Tennessee governmental and political establishment and resulted in multiple indictments. The *Virginian-Pilot's* Tom Turcol won a Pulitzer Prize in 1985 for his investigative reporting in Chesapeake, Virginia; it was the *Pilot's* third Pulitzer.

While Landmark's broadcast division was minuscule compared to other media outlets, KLAS-TV and NewsChannel 5 consistently were at the top of their markets, in large part because of their emphasis on news and local programming. Nashville ranked thirtieth among Nielsen TV markets, for example, but it outperformed all other CBS affiliates in the country in viewership. The president and general manager of both stations are accomplished women and longtime Landmark employees: Emily Neilson at KLAS-TV, and Debbie Turner at NewsChannel 5.

Another Landmark venture can be traced to a team from the Landmark corporate staff that was looking into the classified publications' market nationwide. Readers, the company knew, liked specialty classified magazines. They were easy to scan and full of merchandise from used cars to ukuleles. The publications captured a small but extremely profitable share of the classified advertising market, the bulk of which was traditionally served by metropolitan newspapers.

In November 1985, Landmark acquired *Triad Trading Post* in Winston-Salem, North Carolina, for $1 million. Dick Barry, then president of Landmark, and Bill Diederich, chairman of Landmark Community Newspapers, Inc., recognized that Landmark had to act quickly to find and purchase similar family-owned publications around the country before newspaper companies realized what a good value they were. Landmark quickly ramped up its plans to build an entire division based around classified newspapers. Renamed Landmark Target Media, the venture moved to Norfolk in 1989 under the leadership of Conrad Hall.

Cox Enterprises was buying similar classified publications for its Auto Trader unit but in 1990 decided to sell it. Landmark, the only bidder, offered $145 million. When Cox rejected the bid, Landmark proposed a merger of the two operations. Cox accepted. Each company contributed its collection of classified publications and kicked in approximately $90 million to create the new, equally owned enterprise that it christened Trader Publishing Company. Landmark's Hall was tapped to run the joint operation.

Trader quietly began to add new markets. Its strategy focused on diversifying its markets by providing advertising publications for different products, including used automobiles, boats, motorcycles, heavy equipment, trucks, and personnel recruitment. Trader also adopted a strategy of selling, composing, printing, and distributing the publications almost exclusively through its own facilities. Its growth was swift, with Trader reaching nearly every segment of the classified marketplace. By 1997, Trader had established 329 classified ad publications in 175 markets.

In 1992, Batten purchased the Travel Channel from Trans World Airlines. The cable network, which featured programming about worldwide travel, at the time did not become the success that Batten had hoped. As with the Weather Channel, most cable operators were willing to pay subscriber fees to carry the network. When the FCC passed new regulations making it more difficult for cable companies to pass along rate increases to their customers, cable operators had to choose which networks they were willing to pay to carry. Unlike the Weather Channel, Travel frequently didn't make the cut and the network began losing money.

In 1997, Landmark sold Travel to Paxson Communications, which then sold the network to the Discovery Channel.[3] Ironically, years earlier Batten had declined the opportunity to invest in the Discovery Channel when it was first launching. Batten held onto the Latin America Travel Channel, later sold in 2002, and the London-based Landmark Travel, sold in 2004.

In his seven years as the head of San Jose's KNTV, said Dick Fraim, Batten visited the station only once. It wasn't because he wasn't interested; rather, Fraim said, Batten had so much confidence in his senior executives that he saw no need to micromanage. He wasn't "invisible," as Fraim put it—his style was to delegate.[4]

That was how Batten led his diversified company: He expected his executives to do their work without constant supervision. They, in turn, were attracted to the company because of the degree of autonomy. More often than not, if Batten found good managers with the attributes he valued, he moved them throughout Landmark in various jobs, each with greater responsibility than the last.

At most diversified companies, major decisions are made at the corporate level and passed down to the operating units. At Landmark, the corporate staff worked with individual business units on strategic goals. Budgets were approved and businesses held accountable for meeting financial metrics. Each business unit was expected to deliver superior products to advertisers, readers, or viewers, with above average operating margins.

Many employees made lifelong careers at Landmark because of Batten. They described him as cerebral, high-energy, analytical, modest. Soft-spoken and charismatic, but not profound. Willing to work behind the scenes without seeking credit for himself. If he was ever disappointed in people or a business deal, he rarely lost his temper. At times Batten chose to be a player-coach and relished being in the thick of day-to-day operations, brainstorming business strategies with senior managers, or negotiating a deal. At other times, he kept to the sidelines, preoccupied with industry or civic responsibilities.

Batten's blend of critical thinking, toughness, and compassion helped craft the Landmark culture, according to R. Bruce Bradley, retired president of Landmark's newspapers and a Landmark executive vice president. Bradley shared a list of six qualities with prospective recruits.[5] First, new hires would succeed if they were hard workers who were driven more by a sense of accomplishment than money. Second, honesty and integrity were imperative. Innovation was another common trait at Landmark, Bradley would say, pointing to start-ups Trader, TeleCable, and the Weather Channel. The *Beacon*, a tabloid inserted in the *Virginian-Pilot*, was believed to be the first community paper of its kind in a daily newspaper in the country.[6] There also was a certain understated quality among most Landmark leaders, including Batten. Showiness was not acceptable.

There were few perks. There were no paid country club member-
ships, no corporate dining rooms or gyms. Managers typically did
not fly first class on business trips.[7]

Last, there was a genuine and sincere sense of caring for cowork-
ers. Batten sent hand-written notes to his senior managers thanking
them for jobs well done. Sandra Mims Rowe, editor of the *Orego-
nian* in Portland, Oregon, from 1993 to 2009, earlier led the Norfolk newspapers and said she still has "every note Frank Batten ever
wrote me."[8]

Said Decker Anstrom, former president and chief operating officer of Landmark Communications and chairman of the Weather
Channel: "It's a sense that somehow the family that owns the company actually has an interest in and cares about you as an employee."[9]

At the annual meeting for the company's senior executives, Batten would stand in front of the room and individually welcome by
name and title as many as 100 managers seated in front of him. Batten remembered not only faces but also the job responsibilities of
each key Landmark leader from coast to coast.

Successful Landmark executives also were capable of doing more
with fewer resources. "Do department heads need company cars?"
former Landmark broadcast executive and later chief financial officer Lem Lewis asked rhetorically. "Clearly no. Landmark has prided
itself on being frugal."[10] Batten and former Landmark executive Bill
Diederich set the standard for thriftiness by not turning on the fau-
cets to spend money foolishly just because there was money in the
bank, Lewis pointed out.

Batten's belief in loyalty—in giving a person a job to do and step-
ping back—was emulated by his senior managers with their own
employees. Some thought him loyal to a fault, failing to dismiss mediocre performers. Batten himself believed it his major shortcom-
ing, although it did result in fierce company fealty.

Bob Benson, who at various times was president of Landmark's
three largest daily newspapers, said Batten put people in jobs where
there was no evidence they'd succeed and gave them the opportunity to learn and grow. Early in his career, Benson was the adver-

tising director in Norfolk. Batten called him to his office one day and asked him to take over the newspaper's circulation department. Benson was aware that there was a circulation department "someplace" but that was about the extent of his knowledge. He took the job. "He wanted me to do it so I did it. And the next thing I knew he called me over and said, 'I want you to go to Roanoke to be the president.'"[11]

Carl Mangum, who also had been president and publisher of Landmark's Greensboro and Norfolk newspapers, said Batten led by example. "He was always engaged. He contributed. He listened, but he never took over a meeting. He wasn't interested in promoting himself or taking credit from others."[12]

For Batten, trust was the critical quality of his leadership. "You can't put a price on that, but it is an incredibly valuable asset," Batten told his senior managers in one speech. "Someone we were discussing a risky business venture with told me, 'In the end, the reason we decided to do this with you is that we trust you.' I don't know anything else I would rather hear said about Landmark."[13]

Batten's abilities were recognized by colleagues who sought to merge their companies with his. After his cancer surgery, Katherine Graham asked Batten to merge Landmark Communications with the Washington Post Company and then run the combined organization. "With all my physical problems, I wasn't sure about taking on a new company, a big merger like that," Batten later said. More important, he told Graham, he had no intention of turning Landmark over to anyone. Graham's husband, Phil, years earlier had looked into buying Batten's newspapers outright.

In 1987, Batten was courted by Knight-Ridder in what that publishing group saw as a "dream merger" of the two newspaper operations. Chairman and CEO Alvah H. Chapman Jr. tried to convince Batten to join forces. Chapman wrote to Batten, commending him for his "leadership, business acumen and great stature in (our) industry. . . . The Knights and the Ridders — who, with a few other 'founding family' members and senior executives, own 44% of

Knight-Ridder — would (should a merger be consummated) welcome you as a new and major owner of our company."[14]

The letter, mailed in confidence to Batten's Virginia Beach home, predicted that a merger would yield the "premier company in our industry." Knight and Ridder had merged in 1974, providing stockholders with an annual growth rate of more than 26 percent. "A merger with your company could (in my view) cause that to accelerate," Chapman continued, "both in profit growth and in acceptance in the financial marketplace."

Chapman praised Batten for his leadership "with distinction, with great success, and with both a willingness and ability to serve our industry." In a merger, Batten would be offered a "very senior management involvement," as well as appointment as a director of the Knight-Ridder board, its vice chairman, and chairman of the executive committee. Frank Batten was the only media company owner Chapman ever asked to run Knight-Ridder.[15]

Batten was wooed as well by many other media executives looking to combine assets. None of the offers was attractive to him. "I've *never* considered the idea of selling the company," Batten emphasized. "I wanted to keep the company private."[16]

17 A Transformative Impact

BATTEN AS PHILANTHROPIST

THE IMPORTANCE OF helping others was something Frank Batten learned as a child, when he donated change to the March of Dimes to fight polio and raised money to benefit the newspapers' Joy Fund for needy children. In his lifetime, the amount of his donations would reach more than $400 million, much of it from the sale of TeleCable in 1995.

Despite his contributions, his net worth kept him on the *Forbes* magazine list of the 400 Richest Americans from its inception in 1982. By 2008, when his estimated net worth was $2.3 billion to $2.4 billion, Batten was part of the magazine's "Founder's Club," one of only thirty-one "timeless tycoons" out of 1,300 who had stayed on the list every year—although from the start he had contested *Forbes*'s figures, claiming that its initial estimate of his worth as $140 million was greatly exaggerated, giving him credit for assets not owned by him or his family. *Forbes,* which ranked Batten the 190th-wealthiest man in the country in 2008, described Batten as a "low-profile media maven."[1]

Educational initiatives were the primary beneficiary of his largesse. In 1988, Batten and Josh Darden Jr. read a story in the *New York Times* about a businessman who took a class of Harlem sixth-graders under his wing. Provided they graduated from high school and were admitted to college, he told the children, he'd pay for their college educations. In an inner-city school with a 75 percent dropout rate, 90 percent of this sixth-grade class completed high school, and more than half went on to college. Was there something on a smaller scale that could be done in Norfolk that would benefit its public high schools, Batten and Darden wondered?

Supporting education was a shared passion for the pair. A Norfolk native and a University of Virginia graduate, Darden had served on the university's board of visitors from 1982 to 1990 and was rector during his last three years on the panel. He also helped raise more than $511 million from 1993 to 1997 as chair of the university's seven-year capital campaign, which ended in 2000.

The model the two men chose was the Cleveland Scholarship Program, which provides advisors to help Ohio students apply for college financial aid. To launch the Access College Foundation, Batten and Darden donated a total of $150,000 and found sponsors to make commitments for $1 million. In 2003, Frank and Jane Batten donated $11.2 million to establish the Batten Endowment Fund for Access.

By 2010, the twenty-nine public high schools in Norfolk and four neighboring cities had counselors who'd helped tens of thousands of students qualify for $260 million in aid. Many were the first in their families to attend college and would not have kept going to school if not for the program. In October 2010, the National College Access Network honored the foundation with its first award of excellence.

The opportunity Batten provided was, in turn, a model for others. Donald Graham, chairman of the Washington Post Company, said he had such respect for Batten's judgment that he started the District of Columbia College Access Program.

Throughout his life, Batten gave much of his time, as well as tens of millions of dollars, to Old Dominion University. Roseann Runte, ODU's president from 2001 to 2008, said Batten not only built the foundation for the university's future, but helped each president after its first develop an "agenda of selective excellence."

Batten's impact on the university's oceanography, liberal arts, and engineering departments, as well as its sailing and tennis programs, was transformative. From 1986 to 2006, Batten gave ODU $44 million from his own fortune, Landmark Communications, and the Batten Foundation. When the university launched research in bio-electrics, Batten understood its importance to cancer research and enthusiastically supported it. His gifts created chairs or professorships in engineering, science, music, Jewish studies, real estate, health sciences,

English, psychology, and education. He established programs in creative writing and journalism. In 2003, he made the largest gift in the school's history—$32 million that endowed research and established faculty chairs at all six of the university's academic colleges, with particular emphasis on engineering and science.

In the autumn of 2002, Batten and his five cousins donated the research vessel *Fay Slover* to ODU's Ocean, Earth and Atmospheric Sciences Department. The fifty-five-foot boat, named in honor of his aunt, is based at the National Oceanic and Atmospheric Administration's Marine Operations Center in Norfolk and supports marine science and educational research for the mid-Atlantic states.

During Batten's tenure as rector from 1962 to 1970, the student body more than doubled, from 4,700 to 9,600. The number of faculty grew from 62 to 400. The operating budget mushroomed from $1.8 million to $12.7 million. He helped build a foundation for the school's future growth, which was explosive: By 2010, the campus was home to more than 24,000 students, with 167 undergraduate and graduate degree programs, more than 1,100 full- and part-time faculty, and $96.2 million in research and development expenditures. The College of Arts and Letters building is named after him. Its engineering school is the Frank Batten College of Engineering & Technology.

Private Norfolk Academy benefited from $11 million in gifts from the Battens. Virtually every school in Virginia with the word "Academy" in its title was established as a way of defying integration, but Norfolk Academy was an exception: It was established in 1728. Batten was expelled from the private day school as a youngster but had sent his three children there. More than making up for his own youthful peccadilloes, Batten was a trustee of the school from 1957 to 1982, and president of its board from 1975 to 1979.

The campus library, dedicated in 1995, was named after Batten, who did not want his name attached to the new facility. He was never one for perpetuating his name in bricks and mortar. A campus delegation met with Batten and told him that other buildings on the school's campus were named for leading citizens. Batten had given

$400,000 to the library campaign. Frank Batten Jr. and Dorothy Batten, both graduates of Norfolk Academy, had each contributed $50,000.

The school's request that he lend his name was something Batten could not readily agree to, although six months later, he reluctantly acquiesced. Three weeks before the Batten Library opened, he toured the new facility. He was delighted with what he saw, but he also knew that without continually updated technology, the library would become a dinosaur. As they walked through the building, a modern structure with one curved wall made almost entirely of glass, Batten asked headmaster John H. Tucker Jr., "Would you permit me to create an endowment for technology?"

With an additional $1.1 million gift, Batten created his namesake technology endowment to answer the library's future hardware and software needs. "It was an answer to a prayer," Tucker recalled, "because the operating budget would have been severely affected by attempting to keep up with future costs."[2]

As headmaster, Tucker was encouraged by Batten and other board members to promote the arts. Shortly before his 2000 retirement,[3] board president and former Landmark executive Al Ritter and his wife, Bridget, hosted a farewell party for the headmaster on a balmy June night on the lawn of their Virginia Beach home. At the end of the evening, Batten surprised Tucker with an artist's rendering of a new arts center, to be named after Tucker. To energize a $20 million capital campaign for the center, Batten presented his own $5 million gift in honor of his friend.

Batten's largest beneficiary has been the University of Virginia. Batten had been one of the most ardent supporters of its Darden Graduate School of Business since its inception. He was a trustee and a trustee emeritus of the school, and his son and his daughter Dorothy earned MBAs from Darden. His initial gifts created the Batten Fellowship, an endowed MBA scholarship for journalists and others associated with the media, and the Landmark Communications faculty chair.

The bulk of Batten's $73 million-plus donations to Darden went to support entrepreneurship, a subject close to his heart. Jim Collins, author of *Good to Great*, told Batten that he has always remembered his philosophy that entrepreneurship is not just a start-up concept, or even just a business concept, but a life concept.

Half of all Darden MBA students are expected to go into business for themselves in the decade following graduation, which suited Batten's desire for a program that would benefit both up-and-coming entrepreneurs and corporate innovators, according to C. Ray Smith, a retired business school faculty member.[4] Darden's Batten Center for Entrepreneurial Leadership was born in 1995 with a $10 million gift. The Center morphed into the Batten Institute after he donated an additional $62 million in 1999.

The Batten Institute's mission is to position Darden as the "preeminent educator and thought leader in entrepreneurship and innovation," Batten wrote in a letter to Jeanne M. Liedtka, the Institute's former executive director.[5]

Students focus on the development of emerging and high-growth industries, such as biotechnology and software. The institute extends education beyond the classroom by supporting opportunities for students to join promising start-ups or to start their own companies from scratch. Darden alumni frequently act as outside advisors. The institute also contributes to U.Va.'s efforts to commercialize new technologies and expand the state's biotech base.

Students also learn how mature companies foster innovation on a sustained basis, a relatively unexamined source of potential gain in many companies. Research centers on large, established companies that are successfully growing; the first executive the institute called on to share his insights was Conrad Hall, CEO of Landmark's Dominion Enterprises.

Entrepreneurial ideas become reality in the Batten Institute's Darden Progressive Incubator. A business incubator is an organization or a place that helps entrepreneurs start and establish a business. In exchange for an equity share of the company, traditional incubators provide start-ups with space and access to needed resources. With the Darden Progressive Incubator, space is provided by the university for the new business, but Darden does not take an equity share of the business. Entry to the incubator comes through participation in business plan competitions held by the University of Virginia. Each year, four to eight companies enter the incubator and the same amount "graduate" to new offices and corporate lives.

In April 2007, Batten made his single largest philanthropic donation, giving $100 million to the University of Virginia to establish the Frank Batten School of Leadership and Public Policy. The gift, announced on the university's Founder's Day, also was the largest single gift in the history of the university. And it was the first new school established at U.Va. since 1954 when the Darden business school—to which Batten has donated more than $73 million—was created.

U.Va. president John Casteen said just as Darden focused on corporate leadership, the new Batten School would emphasize national leadership in government, civic affairs, or foundations. Batten's gift, he said, "will both preserve our democratic traditions and inspire the next generation" to live up to university founder Thomas Jefferson's ideals.[6]

The Batten School provides programs in leadership and policy analysis, and fosters research on public issues including poverty, education, and health care in an accelerated, five-year bachelor/master of public policy program. Its first master of public policy class graduated in May 2009. Harry Harding, a China scholar and former dean of the Elliott School of International Affairs at George Washington University, became the school's first dean in July 2009.

If Batten's character was developed at Culver Military Academy, it was Harvard Business School that taught him how to be a business leader. In 2003, Batten donated $32 million to support the ongoing development of the school's residential campus. In recognition of his generosity, the southern, main entrance to the campus was named Batten Way.

The school planned to construct a number of new buildings over the next twenty-five years, adding roughly a half-million square feet of teaching, research, and living space. One of the new buildings was to be named after Frank Batten. The type of building and its use have yet to be determined, said Angela Crispi, associate dean for administration at the business school. "But we know Frank Batten's generosity will enable us to meet the needs of our students and faculty for decades to come."[7]

The business school's growth is part of a long-term Harvard University expansion on more than 200 industrial acres in Boston's Allston neighborhood, which is adjacent to the existing Cambridge campus. Preliminary ideas for the anticipated southward spread over the next half-century were released in January 2007. But by early 2009, Harvard president Drew Faust said the Allston expansion, including construction of a $1 billion science complex, was put on hold.

When the development does take place, the approach to the business school from the south becomes extremely important, said Jay O. Light, dean of the business school's faculty. "Frank Batten's gift," he said, "helps us secure our future."[8] That reality likely will be delayed for the foreseeable future.

Over the years Frank and Jane Batten made two significant contributions to Virginia Wesleyan College, which remain the largest gifts to the Methodist-affiliated school. Jane Batten was a long-time member of the college's board, had served as its chairwoman for three years, and had been a member of Virginia Wesleyan's capital campaign for five years. Frank told Virginia Wesleyan president William T. Greer that he wanted to honor Jane by building a student center.

In February 2002, the $18.6 million, 137,000-square-foot Jane P. Batten Student Center opened. It houses a convocation center that seats 1,500 people, and boasts an eight-lane pool, a grill, a bookstore, meeting rooms, rock-climbing walls, and a 5,000-gallon aquarium. That spring, Frank Batten was the first person to receive an honorary doctorate from the school.

In 2003, drawing on the proceeds from the sale of TeleCable, Batten and his wife contributed $163.7 million to eight educational institutions. In 2006, he donated $1 million to local Tidewater Community College and $2 million to Hollins University for the Batten Leadership Institute. In support of "The Hollins Campaign for Women Who Are Going Places," the Battens in the spring of 2009 gave an additional $3 million to further endow the school's leadership program that bears their name. He donated $20 million for a new Norfolk library to be named after his uncle. The Samuel L. Slover Library is to open in 2013. In a departure from his usual giving, which was directed almost exclusively at education, Batten also contributed $7 million to bring tapirs, lemurs, and gibbons to the Virginia Zoo in Norfolk.

Batten also established the Landmark Foundation as an extension of his own philanthropy and mandated that Landmark businesses give money each year to their local charities. The foundation, begun in 1953, gives away money to nonprofits such as the United Way and Salvation Army, for scholarships, and to various arts and cultural groups. By the autumn of 2010, its endowment had grown to $75 million, even though the foundation continues to donate 5 percent of its value every year. Another charitable trust, the Batten Foundation, had assets valued at $43 million for the tax year ending June 30, 2009. Between the calendar years 2006–2008, the foundation donated $40 million to the University of Virginia, $700,000 to the Colonial Williamsburg Foundation, and $200,000 to Tidewater Community College.

When it came to charity, Batten took a businessman's perspective. He favored major gifts, which he expected would make more of a difference than distributing his kindness in smaller quantities to a multitude of causes. He also chose to give away much of his fortune while he was alive to see it put to use. That also made him an easy target.

Batten was hit up for money constantly. He understood that to raise money, people and organizations had to go where the money was, but he said he was "cold-blooded" about his giving.[9] Spreading his money too far would lessen the impact of his gifts, he believed, so he preferred to give substantial sums to a few beneficiaries. "You have to say no to a lot of people," he said matter-of-factly, "and not worry about it."[10]

18 A Legacy Passed On

On New Year's Day 1998, Frank Batten Jr. succeeded his father as chairman of Landmark Communications, becoming the third generation to lead the family-owned media company. After more than forty years in the saddle, as the elder Batten put it, the time was right to pass the reins. Typical of Landmark's low-key style, no speeches or celebrations marked the occasion.

Batten had known for some time that he had to loosen his hold on the company. Both his daughter Dorothy and his son, Frank Jr., had received MBAs from the University of Virginia's Darden School of Business. Both had experience in the media. After graduating from Hollins University in Roanoke, Dorothy worked in England for Lloyd's of London, and later joined the advertising staff of the *Washington Post*. Between the first and second years of her MBA program, she interned with the Weather Channel's marketing staff in Atlanta. Frank Jr. worked in the *Pilot*'s newsroom as a copy boy. He spent a summer in the paper's circulation department while attending Dartmouth College, where he received a degree in history in 1980. Thanks to his father's position on the board of the Associated Press, young Batten's first full-time job after receiving his MBA in 1984 was one many seasoned reporters only dream of—as an AP correspondent in London.

Dorothy was not interested in working for Landmark. Her father loved the art of the deal. "I don't have a competitive bone in me," she said.[1] Her sister, Leela, described their brother as the perfect son, a "truly good" person who "was sort of born a forty-year-old man, a grown-up."[2] Frank Jr. is thoughtful and literal, self-effacing, private, and spare with his words.

Frank Jr. had not been promised the Landmark chairman's job. He always had been told he would have to earn it. He began his career after college at the *Roanoke Times,* where he worked in the advertising department and in the newsroom. In 1986, after an eighteen-month stint with the AP, he was named general manager, and later publisher, of the *News-Enterprise,* Landmark's community daily in Elizabethtown, Kentucky. Four years later, he moved to the *Virginian-Pilot* and the *Ledger-Star* as marketing director and then as vice president and associate publisher. From 1991 to 1995, he was president and publisher. His last position with Landmark prior to becoming chairman at the age of thirty-nine was as executive vice president with responsibility for new ventures and new media.

Under Frank Jr.'s leadership, Landmark continued to change in response to new opportunities and conditions. Weather Services International was purchased in 2000 for $20 million. The same year, more than $25 million was invested in Great Bridge LLC, a start-up that provided marketing and support for open-source software used to manage databases. Like PostgreSQL and Linux, open-source software is freely owned and updated by programmers worldwide. Though *Fortune* magazine named Great Bridge as one of the "25 Coolest US and Global Companies," it failed to attract the anticipated demand from commercial users and folded the following year. Frank Jr. also presided over the breakup of Trader Publishing and the subsequent creation of Dominion Enterprises, the successor to a substantial portion of the assets of Trader.

In the summer of 2000, Trader, jointly owned with Cox Enterprises, paid $520 million to buy United Advertising Publications, a Texas publisher of real estate magazines, apartment guides, and parenting publications. With that purchase, Trader rounded out its product offerings by providing the two remaining advertising categories found in a newspaper's classified section: real estate for sale and apartments for rent.

As the company matured, however, it became increasingly difficult, and often took far too long, for Cox and Landmark to reach mutually acceptable agreements on operating and strategic issues. Near the end of a fifteen-year partnership, their approach to growth diverged. By September 2005, even though the company's profits were Landmark's second largest after the Weather Channel, classified advertising, which was steadily eroding nationwide, had become a disproportionately large part of Landmark's overall revenues. As the traditional delivery of established news and information also began to unravel, it became clear that it was time to divest at least a portion of Landmark's businesses. Before suggesting a move so bold as to sell the entire company, the younger Batten told his father that Landmark should dispose of its newspapers, its share of Trader Publishing, or both.

In March 2006, Landmark and Cox announced they'd divide Trader between themselves. When the deal was finalized that September, Landmark owned the media and information service properties in the employment, real estate, recreation, and industrial categories; Cox kept the automotive classified advertising businesses. Dominion Enterprises, with revenues estimated at $850 million, in 2007 moved into a new twenty-story office tower in downtown Norfolk. As print advertising and the global economy began to falter, Dominion would begin to have its own challenges.

Meanwhile, the *Virginian-Pilot* became a part of Local News on Cable, a joint venture triumvirate launched in 1997. In September 2006, KLAS became the first television station in Nevada to broadcast local news in high definition. In 2007, NewsChannel 5 was the first in Tennessee to broadcast in HD. Both were among the initial four CBS affiliates nationwide to provide local weather in HD. The Weather Channel invested tens of millions of dollars to switch to HD, no small feat in that the network broadcasts live and around the clock. The Weather Channel Interactive offered not only weather .com but also broadband and wireless weather products, including mobile web, mobile video, and messaging.

Frank Jr. took an active place in the community but preferred to maintain a low profile. He served as rector of Old Dominion University from 2002 to 2004 and as a member of its board for five additional years. He was chairman of Children's Health Foundation of the Children's Hospital of the King's Daughters in Norfolk.

Frank and his son were extremely close. Over lunch every couple of weeks they would talk about strategy, new markets, growth of the company, and management issues. The elder Batten was brought up to date on major developments in Landmark. Colonel Slover did not dispense unsolicited advice or direction. Nor did Frank Sr., who was happy to offer an opinion, but only if requested; when he volunteered suggestions his son said it was done gently.

Frank Jr. controlled Landmark's Class A or voting stock, making him the final arbiter of all business decisions. The elder Batten had passed control of the company on to his son to keep Landmark in the hands of one person. Daughters Dorothy and Leela each had the same number of shares of Landmark Communications as their brother, but in Class B, or nonvoting stock. Dorothy was a Landmark board member.

Another 200 current and retired Landmark executives owned 28 percent of Class B, nonvoting Landmark stock, which they purchased through the Executive Stock Plan. Created in 1967, it was not a traditional stock option plan. Shares were offered to senior managers at a formula price that uses a multiplier of a five-year moving average of operating earnings. By design, the formula rewarded long-term operating performance as opposed to other stock option plans that rewarded short-term stock market performance. If a Landmark manager with stock left the company or retired, the stock was subject to a buy-back option.

Ideally, concentrating control would make it easier to preserve values and standards from decade to decade and from generation to generation. Colonel Slover sold the controlling interest of the *Norfolk Ledger-Dispatch* to two of his senior managers and later regretted that decision.

Frank Jr. codified the company's values in a written form as Landmark Principles. From the Principles, Landmark identified seven core characteristics and twenty-seven behaviors that every Landmark leader was expected to demonstrate. Its leaders were to be ethical, results-oriented, customer-focused, innovative, strategic, and committed to the organization's people and mission. Its leaders were expected to do the right thing, even if it was difficult or unpopular. They were to treat others and their opinions with respect. They were to demonstrate an active concern for people and their needs. The needs and business interests of Landmark were to be put over personal gain.

The core characteristics and behaviors were inspired by the desire to preserve what had made Landmark successful under Colonel Slover and Frank Batten Sr., said Charlie Hill, a Landmark Communications executive vice president, who spearheaded the written policies.

Frank Batten and his son didn't claim to have found any sort of "Eternal Way," the elder Batten said, but they had expected to maintain the company's level of quality and service for at least three generations. But on January 4, 2008, Frank Jr. announced he was selling Landmark Communications' businesses, including its newspapers, TV stations, the Weather Channel, weather.com, specialty publications, electronic media, and other businesses. The decision was his, he said, and had been "emotionally difficult" for him and his father.[3]

The media had changed dramatically in the ten years since he had taken over the company. The industry, prodded by the Internet, was on the cusp of what *Economist* magazine called a communications revolution as profound as Gutenberg's invention of movable type.[4] By 2009, journalism itself was in crisis, declared the president of the American Society of News Editors, and its business model was broken.[5] Even that nonprofit professional group shifted gears, changing its name in March 2009 from its previous American Society of Newspaper Editors.

Daily newspapers and broadcast television, once the mainstay for news and information, were being usurped by the Internet and steadily losing readers and viewers. As the main source of national and international news, only cable TV news channels topped the Web. As readership, advertising, and circulation eroded, the very existence of many large market daily newspapers was threatened. It wasn't an audience or creditability problem, according to the 2009

State of the News Media report, but a revenue problem as advertising decoupled from news.[6]

Newspapers expanded their own Internet sites and scrambled to find new ways to replace lost advertising and circulation. Print classified advertising, in particular, was under pressure as consumers migrated to e-commerce online sites like Amazon, eBay, or Craig's List.

The drop in newspaper revenue initially had been gradual as both print advertising and readership moved to the Internet; its decline was spawned by the worst global recession since the Great Depression of 1929. As the industry sought ways to regain lost revenue, it was as if physical therapy had followed a stroke and suddenly contracted a debilitating secondary illness, wrote the News Media report's authors. Overall, newspaper advertising revenues dipped 41 percent from 2007 to 2009, according to the report's estimates in early 2010.

Newspaper employees, who in the past rarely were concerned about losing their jobs—especially at Landmark—were being laid off, were offered buy-outs, were ordered to take unpaid days off, or had their salaries cut. One out of every five journalists nationwide working for newspapers in 2001 was gone by 2008. Some 5,000 full-time jobs in newspaper newsrooms were axed in 2008 alone. By early 2010, 13,500 jobs for full-time newsroom professionals had disappeared.

Newspaper circulation also continued to drop in 2010, but at a slower pace than the previous year. Average weekday circulation at 635 newspapers declined 5 percent compared to the same six months a year earlier, the *New York Times* reported in October 2010. That compared to a 10.6 percent drop for the same period in 2009.[7] Only the *Wall Street Journal*—the country's largest newspaper—and the *Dallas Morning News* saw an increase in circulation.[8]

Newspapers in larger markets, in particular, struggled with greater competition, too much debt, or unions. Denver's *Rocky Mountain News* and the *Seattle Post-Intelligencer* folded. "Putting on new clothes for a new era," the nonprofit *Christian Science Monitor* ceased publishing a daily print paper and switched to an online product. Others filed for bankruptcy protection to restructure hundreds of millions of dollars of debt, including the Tribune Co., owner of the *Los Angeles Times,* the *Chicago Tribune,* the *Baltimore Sun,* the *Hartford Courant,* and twenty-three television stations; the owners of the *Philadelphia Inquirer,* the *Philadelphia Daily News,* and Philly.com; and the *Minneapolis-St. Paul Star Tribune.* Canada's AbitibiBowater, the world's largest newsprint maker, also filed for bankruptcy protection. Medium and smaller newspapers, such as Landmark's, though battered by the recession, continued to make a profit.

Cable news viewership at Fox News, CNN, and MSNBC was up in 2008, in part because of a presidential election year. By 2009, Fox had surpassed CNN in revenue, profits, and viewership. Fox's primetime viewership on election night in November 2010 was more than triple that of CNN.[9]

Local television advertising revenue dipped 24 percent in 2009, but according to one report, local TV ad revenue was up 13 percent in late 2010 over 2009 and was growing slightly faster than expected.[10] While television remains the largest advertising medium by revenue, the Internet has become the preferred source of information among younger audiences, who shun print publications or network TV. And according to PricewaterhouseCoopers' Global Entertainment and Media Outlook for 2010–2014, the Internet will surpass newspapers as the second-largest advertising medium by revenue.[11]

Frank Batten Jr. belonged to a generation that had seen the advent and astounding commercial growth of the Internet, a global network that began to subsume, and in some cases bury, traditional media. Like his father and great-uncle before him, he felt obligated—at least initially—to carry on the family legacy and hoped his children one day would succeed him. But he didn't share his father's passion for newspapers, nor did he have an emotional investment in the Weather Channel. Frank Jr. did inherit his father's sharp business acumen, a high sense of personal integrity, and a deep understanding of the media business. Their management styles, however, differed.

Frank Sr. was an enthusiastic, emotionally involved "owner operator." If an executive asked him about a thorny problem, he'd eagerly get involved. His son is more quiet and thoughtful. A hands-off executive, he prefers to delegate. His father tended to minimize the risk of intractable adverse trends affecting his businesses. While proud of the company's holdings, Frank Jr. is pragmatic and realistic about their future prospects. He is conscientiously aware of his responsibilities as a fiduciary and strives to serve the interests of Landmark's owners, who include more than 200 active and retired executives of the company.

Though a generation apart, their approach to business was not incompatible until traditional media encountered severe headwinds in the middle of the first decade of this century. While revering his father for having built Landmark during the previous half century, Frank Jr. also recognized that it was his obligation to preserve the value of the company for its owners. He knew it was time to divest.

Certainly the industry today is more competitive and transformative in ways the elder Batten could never have imagined. He and his uncle would have reveled in the challenge to fight the evolving, enigmatic Internet dragon head-on. When he learned of his son's decision to sell the company, all he could do was sit back and hope that it was the best decision for the family and shareholders.

On September 2008, Landmark cashed in on its most valuable and vulnerable asset, the Weather Channel. A consortium of NBC Universal, Bain Capital, and the Blackstone Group signed an agreement to acquire the Weather Channel properties for $3.5 billion. That bought the weather television networks and its ancillary products for radio, newspaper, digital cable services, and interactive television. Also included were the Weather Channel Interactive, consisting of weather.com and products for broadband and wireless platforms; Weather Services International, a business-to-business weather service company for the media, aviation, marine, and energy sectors; and a minority stake in Canadian weather company Pelmorex.

While extremely successful, the Weather Channel was the only major cable network that had no sister networks. Other media companies own multiple cable channels, such as NBC, which also operates MSNBC and CNBC; or ESPN, which has a dozen spinoffs. Cable networks that are part of groups have the benefit of economies of scale; they can offer lower rates to advertisers. The Weather Channel had less clout.

There is little doubt that Frank Jr.'s own two sons will be more inclined to opt for one-stop global shopping, browsing, and news and information gathering on the web rather than listening to a talking head on TV, or wrestling with a newspaper that leaves ink on their fingers. Successors to Kindle and iPad, Facebook, Twitter, blogging, text messaging, and subsequent other application-rich phenomena undoubtedly will be far more attractive to them. Will major daily newspapers even exist? And how will media of the future generate revenue?

The elder Batten regretted the sale, but felt his uncle would have endorsed the idea of parting with the company if it was a good business decision and was best for the shareholders, particularly the controlling owner.

"I understand Frank's rationale," the elder Batten said of his son. "It's just very sad for me because it's meant more than anything else in my life."[12] Had it been his choice, he would not have entertained the idea of selling, and certainly not this soon. That might have been a bad business decision. "I might have waited until too late. Why speculate?" he shrugged as he talked about the sale one afternoon at his Virginia Beach home. "It's really irrelevant. I don't by that mean I'm opposed. Under the circumstances, I think he's doing the right thing. It's very hard for me to think about it. I guess I could say time will tell."

"I'm not running things, and if the management is convinced of it, it's likely to be the right decision," he said. To constrain his son and senior executives would be a mistake, he noted, adding that he "couldn't constrain them anyway."

He was disappointed that his son didn't share his enthusiasm about the Weather Channel. They hadn't talked about that, and he wasn't about to second-guess him. "I can't think for Frank," he said. "I don't know how much of it's a matter of passion and how much is a concern for the future." It is what it is, he mused. He remained optimistic that while newspapers had a strong future, there was no doubt that newspapers also were struggling and "beyond their peak."

"But you know," he said, "that's the way the world and the economy works and to put it simply, the new drives out the old and in time that's good. In this case I can't say it's good because I think there are so many wonderful things about newspapers that have not yet been replaced by new economic developments or new products or new processes." Case in point: Newspapers have the ability to tell stories in depth, or at least more so than contemporary media are able to.

Media watchers had predicted the Weather Channel Networks could fetch as much as $5 billion. Suitors rumored to be interested in what one called "beachfront property" included Time Warner, News Corp., Viacom, and Comcast.[13] Others speculated that Microsoft, Yahoo, or Google also would be tempted. NBC Universal chief executive Jeff Zucker told Harvard students in March 2008 that the Weather Channel's digital properties were "one of the crown jewels" of the Weather Channel.[14]

When the sale of the Weather Channel was consummated in September, Landmark Communications itself was dissolved with the sale of Landmark's stock to the NBC consortium. After twenty-six years on the air, the Weather Channel still was teased for broadcasting weather twenty-four hours a day. The motive behind its sale had been to "create the dullest business partnership in history," joked NBC's Jay Leno on the *Tonight Show.* The Weather Channel was not NBC's first choice, Leno quipped, "but apparently the 'Waiting for paint to dry' channel was already taken."[15]

The nearly 8,000 employees of Landmark's remaining businesses became part of a newly created partnership, Landmark Media Enterprises LLC. Within a month, citing the national credit crunch, the sale of Landmark's NewsChannel 5 broadcast station in Nashville, Tennessee, fell through. Bonten Media Group Inc. had arranged financing with Lehman Brothers, which was being liquidated. Landmark Media Enterprises announced that it was taking all of its properties off the market except the *Virginian-Pilot*. But as the economy worsened, an unnamed suitor for Landmark's flagship newspaper was also squeezed out of a deal in December because it, too, was unable to put together a financial package.

The company's businesses remained open to offers but wouldn't be sold for "several years" until the economy righted itself, according to Landmark Media vice chairman Dick Barry, who retired in June 2010.

Barry said Landmark still intended to sell all of its assets. There was hardly a need for a fire sale. While adversely affected like every other communications company, Landmark Media was better off than most: It was debt-free, and its newspapers, TV stations, Dominion Enterprises, its interactive and other businesses still expected annual revenues to exceed more than $1 billion.

If Frank Batten Jr.'s decision to sell Landmark and the Weather Channel was based on intuition, his farsightedness had paid off. By early 2009, the U.S. subprime mortgage crisis officially pushed the country into a recession as major U.S. financial institutions collapsed, unemployment skyrocketed, the stock market sank, the securities market collapsed with mortgage foreclosures rising 81 percent, banks failed, and the government planned to take over $1 trillion in toxic debt with the help of private investors.

In hindsight, the timing of the Weather Channel's multibillion-dollar divestiture couldn't have been better.

19 Last Years

COMING TO GRIPS with the emotional aspects of retirement was not easy for Frank Batten. Even after his son officially inherited the title of chairman, Batten felt it was his responsibility to keep the company headed on the course he had set decades earlier. Relinquishing control would be, he decided, a gradual process.

That changed in the autumn of 2001. He was hospitalized with pneumonia and slipped into a coma that left him near death. He regained consciousness a week later, partially paralyzed. His doctors reassured him that he'd get movement back in his paralyzed limbs but that it might take months. He was transferred to a Virginia Beach rehabilitation center where, over a span of weeks, he again learned to move his fingers, then his toes, then his limbs.

The experience convinced him that the company might be better off learning to adapt without him. He devoted himself to becoming what he called an "interested observer." Landmark, he said, had to be on its own.[1]

In January 2004 he asked Dick Barry to take over leadership of the philanthropic Landmark Foundation. Two months later, Batten quietly gave up his post as chairman of the Landmark board's executive committee. Eventually, he backed out of every job. That near-fatal illness, along with an earlier bout with shingles that left him with irretrievably damaged nerves behind his right eye and often severe, throbbing pain in his eye and head, affected his balance. His reflexes dulled. His immune system was weakened by lymphoma. If he took too much medication, he was unable to function; too little, and he was in excruciating pain. He was left hunched and twisted. With his body bent thirty degrees at the hips, it was difficult to walk. In the spring of 2004, he fell and broke his neck. He was home-bound, wearing a neck brace for weeks. Two subsequent falls over the months left him with stitches on his face. In October 2007, Batten took another spill, this time breaking a hip; intensive rehab followed.

Batten was not a religious man. He contended that his spiritual beliefs were too disorganized to make them understandable to what he called a "rational" person, although he was comforted during his 2001 illness when his son read the gospels and Psalms at his bedside.

In 2007, the Battens celebrated their fiftieth wedding anniversary not long after thirty friends and family hosted Frank's eightieth birthday at a Virginia Beach restaurant. His and Jane's roles gradually reversed. In his final years, he spent most of his time at home or in rehabilitation or extended-care retirement communities; she was the one who was sought after for service on boards and commissions. Jane was on the boards of Virginia Wesleyan College, the YMCA of South Hampton Roads, Smart Beginnings of South Hampton Roads, and the George Washington Foundation. Later, she was named to the Chesapeake Bay Foundation and was a key advisor to the new Slover Library in Norfolk. Most of the time, she stuck close to his side.

Over the years the couple had enjoyed a house by the ski slopes in Aspen, Colorado, and a condo near Florida's Gulf Stream Golf Club, sailboats, and a collection of art by Albert Bierstadt, Winslow Homer, and Thomas Hart Benton.[2] Now slower-paced days and simpler pleasures began to take precedence. The couple doted on their six grandchildren and Darby, a coal-black Scottish terrier that their daughter Leela gave her mother when her father was critically ill in 2001. The Battens' Virginia Beach home was an unpretentious, two-story brick house on a finger of land overlooking the Lynnhaven River where azaleas bloomed pale pink and white beneath towering loblolly pines. There had never been butlers, private secretaries, chauffeur-driven limos, or lavish parties. When Frank Batten and his friends went to lunch, they split the bill.

His thirty-six-foot Hinckley Picnic Boat, purchased after his retirement and when he could no longer sail because of his infirmities, was hardly a weekend runabout—it cost more than a half-million dollars—but it was a dinghy next to the yachts owned by other billionaires. Conspicuous consumption simply wasn't appealing. "We live in a nice house, we have whatever we want, but we don't have what some people would have if they were in our position," Jane Batten said. "Why would you?"[3]

Accolades were showered on Batten as he entered his final years. In 2006, the College of William and Mary paid tribute with its Lord Botetourt Award, named after colonial Governor Norborne Berkeley, the Baron de Botetourt, credited with establishing the first scholarships given by an American college. The eighty-pound bronze statue of Lord Botetourt was, Batten said, the prettiest award he'd ever received. The Downtown Norfolk Council honored Batten with its first-ever Lifetime Achievement Award. In 2007, he received the Virginia Commonwealth University L. Douglas Wilder School of Government and Public Affairs' Hill-Robinson Expansion of Freedom Award for his work as publisher when the *Virginian-Pilot* newspapers rejected the state's 1950s massive resistance to school integration. In 2009, he was a recipient of the Virginia Press Association Lifetime Achievement Award.

Batten was hospitalized on Christmas Eve 2008, again with pneumonia. With his immune system weakened, Batten contracted methicillin-resistant *Staphylococcus aureus,* or MRSA, an antibiotic-resistant staph infection. He recovered enough to be moved to the health care unit at the Harbor's Edge retirement community in downtown Norfolk.

He was frail, his silver hair slicked back. On the wall was a framed portrait of Darby, painted by daughter Dorothy. Few things pleased him more than when Jane brought the Scottish terrier for a visit.

Batten continued to regret that the Weather Channel, in particular, had been sold. He wasn't about to let on how much he had mourned its loss. "I'm realistic enough to know my motivation and interest is different from others," Batten said. "I've always known the company would be different. I can't control motivations of people in my family. Obviously, this is not what I had hoped would happen. I had hoped people in my family would continue to operate the company successfully and do it with the same kinds of values the company has today. But I'm realistic enough to know that's not likely to happen."[4]

He was inclined to believe that his son would do his best to put Landmark in the hands of responsible new owners. "He has the final say. I guess the best thing to happen is for people to die before companies get changed in radical ways," he said. Did he wish the company had not been put on the market—that the Weather Channel had not been sold before his own death? Yes, he said, "in a selfish sense, I'd say that."[5]

But he knew Landmark wasn't the first media company to have been sold, and it wouldn't be the last. While the global economic crisis hastened the need to reinvent the media, its challenges had been evident to Batten for some time.

In a speech in the spring of 1993, Batten assured Landmark's senior managers that while Landmark's bottom line was fine, "the competitive trends are not worth a damn." Companies that were comfortable and satisfied took the biggest falls, he said. Newspapers and TV stations were steadily losing market share. Batten was prescient: "New technologies will reshape the media business in the next 10 to 15 years. Some of the changes will be revolutionary and will have an enormous impact on how people get information and entertainment."[6]

Fifteen years after that prediction, hundreds of cable channels and multimedia technologies overlapped with print and video. He knew that while the packaging and dissemination of news and information had been altered forever, readers and viewers still wanted to know what was going on across town or around the world. Figuring out how to make money in a new world dominated by technology was another matter. "Looking back on Landmark, I think we've run a long race well," he said in a 1995 speech.[7] The torch was passed to his son three years later.

Landmark Communications, Inc., the Weather Channel, and weather.com were gone. Landmark Media Enterprises had taken their places, and it would likely be years before any of its newspapers, TV stations, or specialty publications were sold. Batten knew he would not be around to see what was in store for future generations. One thing he was certain of: The mission of the media—regardless of format—was still the same—to unceasingly endeavor to provide news accurately, completely, and fairly.

Batten took pains to ensure that the Slover-Batten family largesse would not end when he died. Before her death in 1967, his aunt, Fay Slover, created the Slover Trust, which ultimately is destined to benefit charities throughout South Hampton Roads. The trust expanded significantly, thanks to the growth of Landmark, the $1.5 billion sale of TeleCable, and the $3.5 billion sale of the Weather Channel. Assets from the trust—which are expected to be substantial—eventually will be turned over to the Hampton Roads Community Foundation, among the top 50 community foundations in the nation in assets. The so-called "dynasty trust" will remain in effect for decades until three generations of the family have passed on.

In a complex formula crafted by family attorney Charles Kaufman, the trust is expected to remain intact until about 2066. Fay Slover's five nieces and Frank Batten, her only nephew, were to collect interest income from two-thirds of the trust until their deaths; the Colonel's numerous nieces and nephews were to receive interest from the remaining one-third of the trust until they die. But the principal cannot be distributed to charity until the deaths of the great-nieces and great-nephews who were born prior to Fay Slover's 1967 death—plus an additional twenty-one years.

Depending on long-term ramifications of the recession of 2008, the Slover Trust could swell to more than a billion dollars. Such a gift would be "transformational," said Josh Darden, chairman of the Hampton Roads Community Foundation.[8] When it becomes available, it may be the largest gift ever received by a community foundation in the United States. When the monies are released, the foundation's board will decide how to distribute the revenue generated by these assets.

Batten's children have carried on his tradition of philanthropy as well. Frank Batten Jr. and his wife, Aimee, donated more than $57 million between 2002 and 2009, much of it to Christian schools, churches, and nonprofit Christian organizations. Their foundation had assets of $59.5 million in 2009. Dorothy Batten's foundation has donated to the arts in Charlottesville, to the Amazon Conservation Association, and to the University of Virginia. Her foundation had assets of more than $18 million in 2009. Since 2000, Dorothy has contributed some $7 million to nonprofit causes.

Batten died on September 10, 2009, at Harbor's Edge in Norfolk. He was eighty-two. Nearly 1,300 people, including former governors, mayors, and college presidents, attended a memorial service a week later at Virginia Wesleyan College in the student center named for his wife.

Frank Daniels, former publisher of the *News & Observer* in Raleigh, North Carolina, and a former Landmark board member, praised Batten for being "probably the most respected" newspaperman among his peers.[9] Even those who didn't know him penned notes of appreciation in an online guestbook. "As a news junkie, the weather channel has been part of my daily diet for the past several years. Our many thanks for allowing his accomplishments to touch so many of our lives," said one note signed "Weather Channel Enthusiast." Rob Long, a Hollywood writer and producer, wrote in the *Wall Street Journal* that Batten had created "perhaps the most vanilla of all cable offerings." Yet when sold, it fetched a "very unboring $3.5 billion," which Long called an "amazing sum for a channel with no sizzle, no personality and no sex."

Frank Batten was not a born leader. He lacked confidence. His mother was distant. He had no father. He wanted to please his aunt. He found it disconcerting to measure up to the Colonel, the man who was uncle, father, and grandfather all rolled into one.

Even most of his closest friends saw Batten as aloof, one who may have been a colleague but rarely a buddy. "I'm a very private person and when it comes to personal things, I haven't confided in many people on many occasions," he acknowledged.

Feelings overwhelmed her father, daughter Leela said, and he found it difficult to express them. He loved her. He was proud of her, she said—he just didn't know how to show it. It's a protective mechanism, explained daughter Dorothy before his death. "He has an iron wall around him that he won't unlock." If he did open that door, she said, "he'd be busted."[10] Those who saw him as a successful businessman and entrepreneur—the epitome of self-assuredness and self-control—would find that he struggled throughout his life to prove he was good enough, that a tough exterior shielded a vulnerable side. He was not prone to self-examination. "I can't go that deep into my psyche," he said.

Dorothy said she and her father tended to be disorganized, totally unfocused, disconnected. "Most people didn't see that side," she said. Her father was focused when he knew what he wanted to accomplish. Otherwise? "Totally random and disorganized."

Only by going hundreds of miles away to military school, and exceeding his uncle's reach, did Batten find himself. After Culver he strove to earn the advantages he enjoyed. Because Colonel Slover "sort of handed him everything on a plate," Jane Batten said, her husband "was compelled to demonstrate that he was deserving of the opportunity. He took it and ran with it instead of just kicking back and enjoying being the 'nephew.'"

Batten made a difference in countless thousands of lives, through the Weather Channel, Landmark's newspapers and TV stations, the Associated Press, the cable industry, and colleges and universities, as well as those he helped directly or indirectly by his philanthropy. "It's like throwing a pebble in the water and watching the ever-increasing circles move out," said TeleCable's Dick Roberts.

It's unusual in business for aggressive executives to be revered in their lifetime, noted *New Yorker* columnist and author Ken Auletta. "People are respected for their brains or shrewdness, but rarely do their peers step back and say, 'What a good man.'"[11]

Batten said he wanted to be remembered as a "decent guy" who was straightforward, candid, and friendly. He wanted to be remembered as someone with a conscience, a sense of humor, someone who didn't take himself too seriously and who genuinely cared about people. He wanted people not to forget his principles: "That I built a strong company that was innovative and that operated with high values. That I was a good citizen, provided leadership, and set an example for the communities I served."[12]

A man whose name few recognized, and even fewer knew well, helped change the face of the twentieth-century media.

Beyond that, his legacy was one of helping others achieve what he called valuable purposes and aims in their lives. "My proudest and most rewarding accomplishments," he said, "have been the opportunities I created for others to grow and prosper."

NOTES

Introduction

1. Dan Burke, quoted in Frank Batten, in collaboration with Jeffrey L. Cruikshank, *The Weather Channel: The Improbable Rise of a Media Phenomenon* (Boston: Harvard Business School Press, 2002).
2. Richard Barry, interview by the author, September 29, 2006.
3. Frank Batten, "Investing in the Future: Making Our Mark through Excellence," Landmark managers' meeting, May 1995.
4. Howard Stevenson, interview by the author, May 7, 2004.
5. Frank Batten, "What Is Landmark All About?" Executive stockholders' meeting, April 1978.
6. John O. "Dubby" Wynne, *Academy, a Magazine for Norfolk Academy Alumni and Friends* (Winter 2010), 2.
7. Batten, interview by the author, February 9, 2004. Batten said he thought he had "no business being in the baseball business" because it would have ended up being a distraction and he wouldn't have started the Weather Channel.
8. "Forbes: Value of Yanks now worth $1.6 billion." http://riveraveblues. com/2010/04/forbes-yanks-now-worth-1-6-billion-26434/.
9. John William "Bill" Diederich from the Landmark corporate staff deserved "more credit than anybody else" for steering him to a weather network, Batten said. "Bill had a vision some years before we got into the Weather Channel about how programming and cable would develop. Long before anyone else thought about it, he'd say, 'Some day there will be all-news, all-weather, all-sports channels on cable.' That's when we pursued the idea of an all-news channel." Interview by the author, June 5, 2005.
10. Frank Batten, July 30, 1990, letter to W. Thomas Johnson Jr.
11. "The Founders' Club," Forbes.com, http://www.forbes.com/2002/09/13 /400redistribution_print.html.
12. Batten, interview by the author, June 18, 2004.

1. The Colonel

1. Batten, interview by author, Jan. 8, 2004.
2. Mary Harris, Clinton, Tennessee, July 26, 2006. Goodspeed's History of East Tennessee, Nashville, Tennessee, 1886–1887, 1121. Information available on http://www.tngenweb.org/records/goodspeed.html.

3. Lenoir Chambers and Joseph E. Shank, *Salt Water and Printer's Ink* (Chapel Hill: University of North Carolina Press, 1967), 249.

4. "S. L. Slover Dies; Headed Papers," *Virginian-Pilot*, November 30, 1959.

5. Ibid.

6. Chambers and Shank, *Salt Water and Printer's Ink*, 253.

7. "S. L. Slover Dies; Headed Papers," *Virginian-Pilot*, November 30, 1959.

8. S. L. Slover, Memorandum of Agreement, May 24, 1928. Batten files.

9. Chambers and Shank, *Salt Water and Printer's Ink*, 347.

10. S. L. Slover, Memorandum of Agreement, May 24, 1928.

11. Chambers and Shank, *Salt Water and Printer's Ink*, 346.

12. Chambers and Shank, *Salt Water and Printer's Ink*, 354.

13. Thomas C. Parramore with Peter C. Stewart and Tommy L. Bogger, *Norfolk: The First Four Centuries* (Charlottesville: University Press of Virginia, 1994), 320, 322.

14. Chambers and Shank, *Salt Water and Printer's Ink*, 363.

2. A Life of Privilege

1. Fay Martin Chandler, interview by the author, December 4, 2004. Unless otherwise noted, all subsequent quotations by Fay Martin Chandler are from this interview.

2. Batten, interviews by the author in this chapter, January 7, January 8, January 19, January 27, 2004.

3. Plebe to Commander

1. Alfred Eisenstaedt photo essay, "Boys in Uniform, Culver Teaching Has Military Trappings," *Life*, June 19, 1939, 59–65.

2. Ibid.

3. S. L. Slover, letter to Col. J. W. Henderson, July 11, 1940.

4. Ibid.

5. Colonel W. G. Johnston, September 16, 1940; letter to S. L. Slover.

6. Culver Academic Records, 1940–45.

7. Jim Henderson, chairman of the Culver Education Foundation Board, in a speech honoring Frank Batten at Culver on May 9, 2003. Henderson also was a member of the Landmark Communications Inc. Board of Directors.

8. Colonel W. G. Johnston, January 11, 1941; letter to S. L. Slover.

9. Culver Academic Records, 1940–45.

10. Batten, interview by the author, January 8, 2004.

11. Ibid.

12. Lucius Parkinson, telephone interview by the author, March 10, 2006.

Unless otherwise noted, all subsequent quotations by Lucius Parkinson are from this interview.

13. Culver Academic Records, 1940–45.

14. Batten, interview by the author, January 19, 2004.

15. Batten, interview by the author, January 7, 2004.

16. http://uboat.net.

17. Bud Hillis, telephone interview by the author, March 13, 2006. Unless otherwise noted, all subsequent quotations by Bud Hillis are from this interview.

18. J. Hobart Tucker, quoted in Henderson speech, May 9, 2003.

19. Culver Academic Records, 1940–45.

20. John R. Mars, telephone interview by the author, June 29, 2004.

21. Jane and Frank Batten '45, "Inspiring Culver to New Heights . . . by Example." Culver Annual Report 2009–2010, 9.

22. Batten, interview by the author, January 22, 2004.

4. "Growth through Change"

1. Frank Batten, interviews by the author, January 8, January 17, January 19, January 22, February 12, February 13, June 18, 2004. Unless otherwise noted, all subsequent quotations by Frank Batten are from these interviews.

2. http://www.usmma.edu/about/history/htm.

3. U.S. Navy Ships http://www.ibiblio.org/hyperwar/OnlineLibrary/photos/shusn-no/cve-no.htm.

4. http://en.bremerhaven.de/experience-the-sea/service-infos/city-history/nazi-era-and-second-world-war-in-bremerhaven.24399.html.

5. Henry Burnett, telephone interview by the author, March 28, 2006. Unless otherwise noted, all subsequent quotations by Henry Burnett are from this interview.

6. St. John Bain, telephone interview by the author, April 4, 2006. Unless otherwise noted, all subsequent quotations by St. John Bain are from this interview.

5. Heir Apparent

1. Robert Fair, telephone interview by the author, April 3, 2006.

2. Frank Thompson, telephone interview by the author, April 3, 2006.

3. Frank Batten, interviews by the author, February 13, February 24, February 26, 2004. Unless otherwise noted, all subsequent quotations by Frank Batten are from these interviews.

4. Frank Batten, e-mail to the author, May 11, 2006.

5. Frank Batten, Personal Reference File, Norfolk Newspapers, Inc., undated.

6. Taking Charge

1. Patricia Sullivan, "Management Guru Peter Drucker Dies," http://www.washingtonpost.com/wp-dyn/content/article/2005/11/11/AR2005111101938.html, November 12, 2005.
2. John William "Bill" Diederich, interview by the author, July 12, 1999. Unless otherwise noted, all subsequent quotations by Bill Diederich are from this interview.
3. Edwin Brandt, telephone interview by the author, May 2, 2006.
4. Chambers and Shank, *Salt Water and Printer's Ink*, 381.
5. William T. Leffler Jr., telephone interview by the author, May 2, 2006. Unless otherwise noted, all subsequent quotations by Bill Leffler are from this interview.

7. Putting Down Roots

1. Jane Batten, interview by the author, July 7, 2004. Unless otherwise noted, all subsequent quotations by Jane Batten are from this interview.
2. Robert N. Fishburn, interview by the author, July 13, 2005. Unless otherwise noted, all subsequent quotations by Robert N. Fishburn are from this interview.
3. Frank Batten, interview by the author, March 8, 2004. Unless otherwise noted, all subsequent quotations by Frank Batten are from this interview.
4. Frank Batten Sr. was a "junior," but because his father died when he was a toddler, he dropped the suffix. He named his own son Frank Batten Jr. When the younger Batten had his own child, he went back to the correct order of the suffixes and named the boy Frank Batten IV.
5. *Norfolk Ledger-Dispatch*, June 11, 1957.
6. Queen Elizabeth II and her husband, the Duke of Edinburgh, visited Jamestown for the 350th anniversary in 1957; it was the first time a reigning British monarch had set foot in the American colonies. In May 2007, the couple returned to Jamestown for its 400th anniversary. Tony Germanotta, *Virginian-Pilot*, November 16, 2006.
7. Parramore, Stewart, and Bogger, *Norfolk: The First Four Centuries*, 333.
8. Alexander S. Leidholdt, *Standing before the Shouting Mob: Lenoir Chambers and Virginia's Massive Resistance to Public-School Integration* (Tuscaloosa: University of Alabama Press, 1997), 62.

8. Taking a Stand

1. Leidholdt, *Standing before the Shouting Mob*, 6.
2. Leidholdt, *Standing before the Shouting Mob*, 64.
3. Ira M. Lechner, "Massive Resistance: Virginia's Great Leap Backward," *Virginia Quarterly Review* (Autumn 1998), http://www.vqronline.org/ articles/1998/autumn/lechner-massive-resistance-virginias/.
4. Lechner, "Massive Resistance: Virginia's Great Leap Backward."
5. Virginia General Assembly, Extra Session 1956, u2.gmu.edu:8080/ dspace/bitstream/1920/2340/2/mann_43_05_02B.pdf.
6. Leidholdt, *Standing before the Shouting Mob*, 75.
7. Leidholdt, *Standing before the Shouting Mob*, 76.
8. Guy Friddell, "Lenoir Chambers: The Schools Open," *Virginian-Pilot*, September 23, 1990.
9. Obituary of Hon. Walter E. Hoffman, *Pennsylvania Gazette*, University of Pennsylvania, November 21, 1966, http://www.upenn.edu/ gazette/1197/1197obits.html#090s.
10. "The Cost of Resistance," editorial, *Ledger-Dispatch*, August 23, 1956.
11. Leidholdt, *Standing before the Shouting Mob*, 79.
12. Leidholdt, *Standing before the Shouting Mob*, 91.
13. Forrest R. White, *Pride and Prejudice, School Desegregation and Urban Renewal in Norfolk, 1950–1959* (Westport, Conn.: Praeger, 1992), 192.
14. White, *Pride and Prejudice*, 201.
15. Leidholdt, *Standing before the Shouting Mob*, 111.
16. Frank Batten, interviews by the author in this chapter, February 12, April 1, April 2, April 20, June 30, 2004; June 2, 2005.
17. White, *Pride and Prejudice*, 210.
18. White, *Pride and Prejudice*, 233.
19. "A New Clear Voice Speaks in Norfolk," editorial, *Virginian-Pilot*, January 27, 1959.
20. Harvey Lindsay, interview by the author, July 1, 2004.
21. Leidholdt, *Standing before the Shouting Mob*, 7.
22. Ibid.
23. Jack Rixey, interview by the author, June 17, 2004.

9. Branching Out

1. John William "Bill" Diederich, interview by the author, July 12, 1999.
2. R. L. Beall, *Greensboro News & Record* history, internal document, July 2006.
3. Batten, *The Weather Channel*, 28.
4. Frank Batten, interview by the author, March 12, 2004. Subsequent quo-

tations in this chapter are from interviews conducted with Frank Batten on April 1, April 29, May 12, May 24, June 17, 2004; March 11, June 2, June 5, June 8, 2005; September 28, 2006.

5. Beall, *Greensboro News & Record* history, internal document. July 2006.

6. Landmark Communications Board of Director minutes, 1965, e-mail. Susan Smith Goetz, September 26, 2006.

7. Most of the unions were simply trying to maintain their union status, especially the pressmen, who liked to flex their muscles, recalled assistant general manager Dick Hendricks. Unions were a way of life. They were a tradition. His own father had been a farmer, just as his grandfather and great-grandfather before him. It was the same way with unions. "You wanted your son to be in the union, so you hired him." Interview with the author, July 21, 2006.

8. Katherine Graham, *Personal History* (New York: Vintage Books, 1997), 541.

9. Ibid., 560.

10. Bud Dashiell, interview by the author, July 31, 2004.

11. Batten, *The Weather Channel*, 19.

12. Gordon Herring, telephone interview by the author, July 7, 2006. Unless otherwise noted, all subsequent quotations by Gordon Herring are from this interview.

13. Nick Worth, interview by the author, May 4, 2004.

14. George Hebert, telephone interview by the author, November 9, 2006.

15. Page Lea, interview by the author, May 4, 2004.

16. Barney Oldfield, interview by the author, May 4, 2004.

17. Dick Roberts, interview by the author, March 31, 2004.

18. Ibid.

19. Jim Robbins, telephone interview by the author, August 18, 2006.

20. Ibid.

21. Gail Sermersheim, telephone interview by the author, August 18, 2006.

22. Bob Fishburn, interview by the author, July 15, 2005. Unless otherwise noted, all subsequent quotations by Bob Fishburn are from this interview.

23. M. William "Bill" Armistead III, interview by the author, October 25, 1999.

24. Walter Rugaber, telephone interview by the author, May 6, 2005.

10. Legal Challenges

1. Richard C. Bayer, "$9 Million in Assets in Sight," *Ledger-Star*, March 3, 1975.

2. Harry Williams, "Ex-Norfolk Savings' Chief to Begin Embezzlement Term," *Virginian-Pilot*, March 8, 1977.

3. Jack Dorsey, "Receiver Responds in Loan Case," *Virginian-Pilot*, August 14, 1974.

4. Don Hill, "Landmark Held Liable; $2 Million Awarded," *Ledger-Star*, February 5, 1975.

5. Don Hill, "Batten Testifies in Landmark Case," *Ledger-Star*, February 4, 1975.

6. Hill, "Landmark Held Liable; $2 Million Awarded," *Ledger-Star*, February 5, 1975.

7. Richard C. Bayer, "Landmark Lawyers File Memorandum," *Ledger-Star*, February 19, 1975.

8. Bill McAllister, "$6.6 Million 'Settlement' in Loan Suits," *Virginian-Pilot*; March 3, 1975.

9. Frank Batten, interview by the author, September 28, 2006.

10. Sarah Huber, telephone interview by the author, October 7, 2006.

11. Kay Mills, *Changing Channels: The Civil Rights Case That Transformed Television* (Jackson: University Press of Mississippi, 2004), 4.

12. "Group Seeks Channel 3," *Ledger-Star*, September 3, 1969.

13. Don Hill, "Favoritism to VNB Charged," *Virginian-Pilot*, May 25, 1972.

14. Don Hill, "Proposed TV Official 'Fired,'" *Virginian-Pilot*, June 2, 1972.

15. Don Hill, "WTAR Target of Witnesses at Public Hearing on License" *Virginian-Pilot*, August 2, 1972.

16. Ibid.

17. Don Hill, "FCC Judge Reaffirms Decision on WTAR-TV" *Virginian-Pilot*, January 24, 1975.

11. A Good Race

1. Frank Batten, interview by the author, March 19, 2004. Subsequent quotations in this chapter are from interviews conducted with Frank Batten on January 23, March 10, and March 29, 2004.

2. Bill Robinson, "First Foreign Winner," *Yachting*, August 1972, 40.

3. Mort Clark, interview by the author, April 12, 2004. Unless otherwise noted, all subsequent quotations by Mort Clark are from this interview.

4. Tom Hunnicut, interview by the author, July 15, 2004.

5. Stephen G. Kasnet, telephone interview by the author, October 10, 2004.

6. Donald H. Patterson Jr., interview by the author, July 28, 2004.

7. Conrad Hall, interview by the author, June 14, 2004.

8. Billy Hunt, interview by author, October 13, 2004.

12. A Temporary Silence

1. Jack Stokes, e-mail to the author, November 13, 2010.
2. "China becomes world's second-largest economy," Bloomberg News, *Financial Post*, http://www.financialpost.com, August 16, 2010.
3. "Major Foreign Holders of Treasury Securities," U.S. Treasury, http://www.ustreas.gov/tic/mfh.txt, October 18, 2010; James Thompson, "China 'Overtakes' Germany to Become Largest Exporter," *Independent*, http://www.independent.co.uk/, January 11, 2010.
4. John Vidal, "UN Report: World's Biggest Cities Merging into 'Mega-regions,'" guardian.co.uk, http://www.guardian.co.uk/world/2010/mar/22/un-cities-mega-regions, March 22, 2010.
5. Frank Batten, interview by the author, April 28, 2004. Subsequent quotations in this chapter are from interviews conducted with Frank Batten on February 25, March 10, April 2, June 14, 2004; July 7, 2005.
6. While he was hospitalized, one of his roommates was Robert Penn Warren. The author had broken his leg on his first day skiing, Batten recalled, and read no fewer than ten books in the hospital, including Whittaker Chambers's lengthy book *Witness*. Frank Batten, interview by the author, February 14, 2004.
7. Stanton Cook, telephone interview with the author, March 26, 2007.
8. John Roderick, "Looking at the New China," *AP World*, no. 1, 1979.
9. Betty Moore, interview by the author, May 17, 2005.
10. Dr. Gary Schechter, telephone interview by the author, March 18, 2004.
11. Matt Clark and Deborah Witherspoon, "Remaking the Human Voice," *Newsweek*, June 21, 1982.
12. Kay Graham. The letter to Frank Batten is undated.

13. Broadening Impact

1. Louis Boccardi, interview with the author, August 20, 2004. Unless otherwise noted, all subsequent quotations by Louis Boccardi are from this interview.
2. Letter to Keith Fuller, AP president and general manager, June 16, 1982.
3. Ibid.
4. Frank Batten, "Financing the Associated Press," November 10, 1982.
5. Kay Mills, *A Place in the News: From the Women's Pages to the Front Page* (New York: Dodd, Mead and Company, 1988), 151.
6. Andrew Radolf, "Batten leaves AP in good shape," *Editor & Publisher*, May 2, 1987.
7. Terry Anderson, telephone interview by the author, July 12, 2006.

8. Frank Batten, prepared speech, Associated Press annual meeting, New York, May 4, 1987.

9. Dave Tomlin, telephone interview by the author, April 2, 2004.

14. "A Preposterous Concept"

1. Kathy Lane, interview by the author, January 20, 2005.

2. Al Lipson, telephone interview by the author, October 30, 2006.

3. Gary Deeb, "Gary Deeb Column on the Weather Channel," Field Enterprises, Inc., July 6, 1983.

4. Batten, *The Weather Channel*, 50.

5. Batten, *The Weather Channel*, 127.

6. Batten, *The Weather Channel*, 126.

7. Bill Matley, interview by the author, January 19, 2005.

8. John Coleman, "Coleman Wins," internal memorandum to the Weather Channel staff, June 29, 1983.

9. Dick Barry, interview by the author, December 12, 2004. Unless otherwise noted, all subsequent quotations by Dick Barry are from this interview.

10. Louis Ryan, interview by the author, January 7, 2005.

11. The law firm changed its name in 2010 from Willcox & Savage to Willcox Savage.

12. Phillip Couri, interview by the author, January 10, 2005.

13. Thomas G. Johnson Jr., interview by the author, December 28, 2004.

14. John O. "Dubby" Wynne, interview by the author, January 5, 2005.

15. Rebecca Beach Smith, interview by the author, September 13, 2006.

16. *Communications Daily*, July 25, 1983, quoting analyst Tony Hoffman.

17. "Coleman Loses Post, Stake in Landmark Communications Inc.," *Wall Street Journal*, August 16, 1983.

15. The Weather Channel Takes Off

1. John O. "Dubby" Wynne, interview by the author, January 4, 2005. Unless otherwise noted, all subsequent quotations by Dubby Wynne are from this interview.

2. Robert Simpson, telephone interview by the author, January 21, 2008.

3. Debora Wilson, e-mail to the author, September 5, 2007.

4. Debora Wilson, interview by the author, March 9, 2007.

5. Frank Batten, interview by the author, May 27, 2003.

6. Batten, *The Weather Channel*, 177.

16. Landmark Continues to Grow

1. Bob Stoldal, e-mail to the author, March 17, 2009.
2. Frank Batten, "The Power of the Press: Maintaining the Public's Trust," October 1984, from "Landmark Communications: A Commitment to Innovation and Excellence, 10 speeches." Unpublished Landmark booklet.
3. Scripps Networks Interactive in 2009 acquired a 65 percent interest in the Travel Channel from Cox Communications for about $1 billion. Cox Communications retained a 35 percent interest. "Scripps Closes Travel Channel Deal," December 15, 2009. http://www.multichannel.com/article/440504-Scripps_Closes_Travel_Channel_Deal.php.
4. Dick Fraim, telephone interview by the author, October 26, 2006.
5. R. Bruce Bradley, interview by the author, May 25, 2005.
6. Frank Batten, interview by the author, April 2, 2004.
7. Batten's annual personal salary was $325,000 in 1998 and $200,000 in 1999. Between 2000 and 2004, his salary averaged $151,000 a year. Landmark internal note.
8. Earl Swift, "Frank Batten," *Virginian-Pilot*, September 11, 2009.
9. Decker Anstrom, interview by the author, June 20, 2005.
10. Lemuel Lewis, interview by the author, January 10, 2007.
11. Bob Benson, interview by the author, November 30, 2005.
12. Carl Mangum, interview by the author, April 14, 2004.
13. Batten, "Investing in the Future: Making Our Mark through Excellence," May 1995, from "Landmark Communications: A Commitment to Innovation and Excellence, 10 speeches."
14. Alvah Chapman, personal letter to Frank Batten, January 19, 1987.
15. Alvah Chapman, telephone interview by the author, October 8, 2004.
16. Frank Batten, interview by the author, June 24, 2004.

17. A Transformative Impact

1. "Relentlessly Rich," *Forbes*, September 11, 2008, http://www.forbes.com/forbes/2008/1006/222.html.
2. John Tucker, telephone interview by the author, December 7, 2006.
3. Tucker was succeeded by Dennis G. Manning as headmaster.
4. C. Ray Smith, interview by the author, November 2, 2005. Unless otherwise noted, all subsequent quotations by C. Ray Smith are from this interview.
5. Jeanne Liedtka, telephone interview by the author, January 17, 2007.
6. John Casteen, telephone interview by the author, May 14, 2007. Casteen retired in 2010; he was succeeded by Teresa A. Sullivan, former provost and executive vice president for academic affairs at the University of Michigan.

7. Angela Crispi, interview by the author January 18, 2007.

8. Jay Light, "Batten Gift to Support Residential Campus," *HBS Alumni Bulletin*, October 5, 2004. http://www.alumni.hbs.edu/bulletin/2003/june/campaign_batten.html.

9. Frank Batten, interview by the author, January 22, 2003.

10. Ibid.

18. A Legacy Passed On

1. Dorothy Batten, interview by the author, November 21, 2006.

2. Leela Bavana, interviews by the author, September 8, 2004; by telephone, August 10, 2004; March 1, 2007.

3. Frank Batten Jr. e-mail to author, June 1, 2009.

4. "What Sort of Revolution?" *Economist,* April 22, 2006.

5. Gregory Favre, "Kaiser Takes Over as ASNE President: 'Our Profession is in Crisis,'" April 27, 2009. PoynterOnline, http://www.poynter.org/column.asp?id=101&aid=162590.

6. "2009 State of the News Media," Pew Project for Excellence in Journalism, http://www.stateofthemedia.org/2009/chapter%20pdfs/COMPLETE%20EXEC%20SUMMARY%20PDF.pdf. Unless otherwise noted, all subsequent quotations are from the report or its subsequent "2010 State of the News Media" at http://pewresearch.org/pubs/1523/state-of-the-news-media-2010.

7. Jeremy W. Peters, "Newspaper circulation falls broadly but at slower pace," the *New York Times*, http://mediadecoder.blogs.nytimes.com/2010/10/25/newspaper-circulation-falls-broadly-but-at-slower-pace/, November 12, 2010.

8. Associated Press, "Newspaper Circulation Slips; Journal Up 1.8%," *Wall Street Journal*, October 26, 2010.

9. Andrea Morabito, "Fox News Tops Election Night Viewership," Broadcasting & Cable, http://www.broadcastingcable.com/article/459376-Fox_News_Tops_Election_Night_Viewership.php, November 3, 2010.

10. "Local TV Advertising Spending up 13 Percent in 2010, BIA/Kelsey Reports," BroadcastEngineering, http://broadcastengineering.com/hdtv/local-advertising-up-biakelsey-0921/, September 21, 2010.

11. Lauren Goode, "Internet Is Set to Overtake Newspapers in Ad Revenue," *Wall Street Journal* blogs, "Digits," June 15, 2010. http://blogs.wsj.com/digits/2010/06/15/internet-is-set-to-overtake-newspapers-in-ad-revenue/.

12. Frank Batten, interview by the author, June 24, 2008. Unless otherwise noted, all subsequent quotations by Frank Batten are from this interview.

13. Andrew Ross Sorkin, "Chain Said to Seek Bids for Weather Chan-

nel," January 3, 2008. http://www.nytimes.com/2008/01/03/business/media/03weather.html.

14. Brian Stelter, "The Web? The Weather Channel Decides to Do Something about It," March 13, 2008. nytimes.com: http://mediadecoder.blogs.nytimes.com/2008/03/13/the-web-the-weather-channel-decides-to-do-something-about-it/.

15. Kristi E. Swartz, "Leno Dryly Sums up Weather Channel's Sale," *Atlanta Journal-Constitution*, July 9, 2008.

19. Last Years

1. Frank Batten, interview by the author, February 26, 2004.

2. The paintings are now on loan to the Chrysler Museum in Norfolk.

3. Jane Batten, interview by the author, July 7, 2004. Unless otherwise noted, all subsequent quotations by Jane Batten are from this interview.

4. Frank Batten, interview by the author, June 24, 2008.

5. Ibid.

6. Batten, "Landmark's Vision: to Become the Leader in All Our Markets," May 1993, from "Landmark Communications: A Commitment to Innovation and Excellence, 10 speeches."

7. Batten, "Investing in the Future: Making Our Mark through Excellence," May 1995, from "Landmark Communications: A Commitment to Innovation and Excellence, 10 speeches."

8. Josh Darden, interview by the author, June 28, 2004.

9. Philip Walzer, "Frank Batten Remembered as 'Low-key' yet 'Extraordinary'" *Virginian-Pilot*, September 18, 2009.

10. Dorothy Batten, interview by the author, November 21, 2006.

11. Ken Auletta, e-mail to the author, November 17, 2006.

12. Frank Batten, interview by the author, June 8, 2005.

INDEX

*Page references to the photo gallery
appear in the following form:* photo
gallery, 6, 8. *Numbers refer to the un-
numbered pages of the gallery, which
appears in the printed book following
page 76.*

Abrams, Stephanie, 132
Access College Foundation, 146–47
Almond, J. Lindsay, Jr., 63–65,
 67–70, 74
Anderson, Terry, 118
Anne, Princess (of England), 118–19
Anstrom, Decker, 143
AP. *See* Associated Press
Armistead, M. William, III, 87–88,
 94
Associated Press (AP), 4, 107–9,
 114–19
Astor, Lady Nancy, 40–41
Auletta, Ken, 171

Babalas, Peter K., 97
Back Bay National Wildlife Refuge,
 18
Bain, St. John, 39
Baldwin, Kenneth W., Jr., 80
Ban, Ray, 121
Barry, Richard F., III, 2, 124–27, 140,
 164, 165
Bass, Preston, 27
Batten, Aimee (daughter-in-law),
 170; *photo gallery, 9*
Batten, Dorothy Martin (mother),
 14, 18–19, 25, 27, 91; *photo gallery, 1*

Batten, Dorothy Neal (daughter),
 58, 149, 154, 157, 170; *photo gallery,
 6, 8*
Batten, Frank: academic challenges/
 successes of, 19–20, 23–30, 29, 148;
 awards and recognitions, 26–27,
 31, 167; childhood and youth of,
 14–32, 100; college experiences
 of, 37–39, 44–46; community
 involvement of, 58, 89–91; as copy
 boy and reporter, 42–44; European experiences of, 35–36, 39–
 41; last illnesses of, 165–66, 170;
 leadership of, 4–5, 30, 46, 86, 117,
 141–44; and Merchant Marine,
 33–35, 37; philanthropy of, 5, 17,
 30–31, 146–53, 169; photographs
 of, *photo gallery, 2–8, 10–12*; political attitudes of, 91; and sailing,
 35; and throat cancer, 5, 106–7,
 109–13; wedding and marriage
 of, 56–57. *See also* Landmark
 Communications
Batten, Frank (father), 14; *photo
 gallery, 1*
Batten, Frank, Jr. (son), 57, 111; community involvement of, 156; early
 career of, 154–55; leadership of,
 160–61; philanthropy of, 149, 170;
 photographs of, *photo gallery, 6,
 8–9*
Batten, Frank, IV (grandson), *photo
 gallery, 9*
Batten, James (grandson), *photo
 gallery, 9*

Batten, Jane (wife), 56–57, 100–101,
152, 166; *photo gallery, 5–6, 8–9*
Batten, Mary Elizabeth "Betsy"
(Leela) (daughter), 58, 154, 157;
photo gallery, 6
Batten Fellowship (U.Va.), 149
Batten Foundation, 153
Batten Institute (U.Va.), 150
Batten Scholarship, 31
Bavana, Maitri Leela. *See* Batten,
Mary Elizabeth "Betsy" (Leela)
Beacon, 142
Beckley (W. Va.), 82
Benson, Bob, 143–44
Blom, Eric, 112
Boccardi, Louis D., 115–18
Bradley, R. Bruce, 142
Bradley, Rex, 82
Brandt, Edwin, 53
Brinkley, Stan, 103
Brown, Ray, 102
Bryan, Joseph, 9
Burke, Dan, 1
Burnett, Henry, 38–39
Bush, Peter B., 79
Byrd, Harry F., 63, 65, 76

cable television industry, 2, 81–84,
122, 160; international, 134–35
Campbell, Gordon E., 96–97, 99
Cantore, Jim, 122, 132
Carlton, Joan, 138
Carpenter, Mike, 26–27
Casteen, John, 151
Chambers, Joseph Lenoir, Jr., 62,
66–68, 70–71, 74–76
Chandler, Alfred, 44
Chandler, Fay Martin, 44–45
Chapman, Alvah H., Jr., 144–45
China: AP mission to, 107–9
Clark, Morton, 102, 106

classified publications market,
140–41
CNN (television network), 5, 122,
160
Coleman, John, 1–3, 120–27; *photo
gallery, 10*
Collette, Mattu, 14, 36
Collins, Jim, 150
Colonial Williamsburg Foundation,
153
Cook, Stan, 81, 108, 109
Couri, Phillip E., 125, 127
Cox Enterprises, 140–41, 155–56
Crispi, Angela, 152
Culver Military Academy, 21, 31

Daniels, Frank, 170
Darden, Colgate, 110
Darden, Josh, Jr., 146–47, 169
Darden, Pretlow, 69, 72–73
Darden Graduate School of Busi-
ness (UVa.), 149–51
Darden Progressive Incubator,
150–51
Dashiell, R. G. "Bud," 81
Delta Kappa Epsilon, 38
Deng Xiaoping, 108–9
Diederich, John William, 53, 140,
143, 173n9
Discovery Channel, 141
Dominion Enterprises, 155–56
Drucker, Peter, 51
Duckworth, W. Fred, 68, 70, 73,
76

Edwards, Bruce, 122
Eisenhower, Dwight D., 72, 74
ESPN (television network), 122
Evening Dispatch, 10
Evening Times-Herald, 9
Executive Stock Plan, 157

Fair, Robert R., 45
False Cape Gunning Club, 18
Fay Slover (research vessel), 148
Federal Communications Commission (FCC), 83, 96–97, 99
Ferguson, Homer L., 44
Fishburn, J. B., 87
Fishburn, Robert N., 56–57, 87
Forbes, 146
Fox News, 160
Fraim, Dick, 138, 141
Frank Batten School of Leadership and Public Policy, 151
Fuller, Keith, 108; *photo gallery, 10*

Galax Gazette, 86
Galumbeck, Alan, 130
Gibbons, Jim, 88
Gietz, William A., 98
Goodloe, Paul, 132
Gould, Wilbur James, 110
Graham, Donald, 147
Graham, Katherine, 81, 108, 112–13, 117, 144
Grandy, Albert H., 12
Gray, Garland, 64
Gray Plan, 64
Great Bridge LLC, 155
Greensboro Daily News, 78
Greensboro News Company, 78–81, 86
Greensboro Record, 78
Gregory, L. Cameron, 52

Hall, Conrad, 105, 140–41, 150
Hall, Leon C., 93
Hampton Roads Community Foundation, 169
Hampton Roads Television Corp., 96–99
Hanes, Tom, 56

Harding, Harry, 151
Hartman, Robert B. D., 28
Harvard Business School, 151–52
Hebert, George J., 83
Henderson, Jim, 174n7
Hendricks, Dick, 79
Herring, Gordon, 85, 130
high definition broadcasting, 131, 156
Hill, Charlie, 158
Hillis, Elwood H. "Bud," 28
Hirohito, Emperor of Japan, *photo gallery, 11*
Hoffman, Walter E. "Beef," 65–67, 71
Hogan, Hunter, 56, 88
Hollins University, 152–53
Holtz, Edgar W., 98
Huber, Paul S., Jr., 48–49, 79, 92–96, 98
Huber, Paul S., Sr., 11, 47
Huber, Sarah, 96
Hughes, Howard, 137–39
Hunnicut, Tom, 103
Hunt, Billy, 105
hunting clubs, 18
Hussein, King of Jordan, *photo gallery, 9*

International Naval Review (1957), 58–60
Internet, 158, 160
investigative reporting, 139–40

Jaffe, Louis, Sr., 63
Jako, Gezo, 111
Jeffress, Charles O., 78
Jeffress, Edwin Bedford, 78
Jeffress family, 78–79
Johnson, Thomas G., Jr., 19, 126
Jones, Thomas D., 94

Kaltenborn, H. V., 17
Kasnet, Stephen G., 104
Kaufman, Charles, 12, 49, 50–51, 60, 72, 169
Keneely, Bill, 121
Kilpatrick, James J., 64
Kissinger, Henry, 118
Kitchin, Lee, 97–98
KLAS-TV, 137–40, 156
Knight Newspapers, 88
Knight-Ridder Newspapers, 137, 144–45
KNTV, 137, 141
Kraushaar, David I., 98–99

labor unions, 80–81
Landmark Communications, 3; beginning of, 83; expansion of, 137–45; lawsuits involving, 92–99, 123–24, 137; principles of, 157–58; sale of, 158, 162–63; stock distribution in, 157. See also Weather Channel
Landmark Foundation, 153, 165
Landmark Media Enterprises, 164
Landmark Target Media, 140
Lane, Kathy, 121
Larson, R. K. T. "Kit," 56
Lea, Page, 84
Leffler, William T., Jr., 54–55
Leno, Jay, 163
Leslie, Joseph A., Jr., 62, 66, 68, 70–71, 75–76
Letterman, David, 122
Lewis, Frederick, 10–11, 47
Lewis, Henry S., 47–48
Lewis, Lemuel E., 139, 143
Lewis, Mary, 11
Light, Jay O., 152
Lindsay, Harvey, 74–75

Lipson, Al, 122
Local News on Cable, 156
"Local on the 8s," 131
Long, Rob, 170
Lugie (nanny), 14
Lustig, Wayne E., 97, 99
Lyons, Steve, 132

MacArthur, Jean Faircloth, 118–19
MacKethan, Edwin R., 93–94
Malone, John, 86
Mancuso, Mark, 121
Mangum, Carl, 144
Mars, John R., 30
Martin, Alvah H., 10
Martin, Dorothy. See Batten, Dorothy Martin
Martin, Fay. See Slover, Fay Martin
Martin, Roy B., Jr., 70
Mason, Bob, 75
massive resistance. See school desegregation
Matley, Bill, 124
May, Ken, Jr., 121
McElwain, Ken, 39
McKinney, Charles, 25
McNeal, H. P., Jr., 21
McNeal, Sonny, 21
Moore, Betty, 111
Morgan, J. P., 8
Morris, Barton W., 87
Morrow, Jeff, 132
Murdoch, Keith "Rupert," 118–19, 135

Neilson, Emily, 140
Newhouse, Donald, 78
Newhouse, S. I., Jr., 78
Newport Bermuda race (1972), 101–3

News & Record (Greensboro, N.C.), 78

NewsChannel 5, 139–40, 156, 164

News-Enterprise (Elizabethtown, Ky.), 155

newspaper industry, 8–9, 42–43, 158–60; circulation promotions in, 16–17; labor unions and, 80–81; ownership regulation and, 99; personnel practices and, 51–52, 80; technology of, 80. *See also* Associated Press; *specific newspapers (e.g,* Virginian-Pilot)

New York Yankees (baseball team), 5, 18

Norfolk (Va.): economic conditions in, 12–13, 59; school desegregation and, 4, 62–72

Norfolk Academy, 20, 148–49

Norfolk Dispatch, 10

Norfolk Ledger-Dispatch, 10–12, 16–17, 47–49, 53–54, 157; school desegregation and, 62, 64–68, 70–71, 76

Norfolk Pilot, 12

Norfolk Public Ledger, 9–10

Norfolk Savings & Loan Corp., 92–96

Norfolk Tars, 18

Northern, Sam, 59

Old Dominion University, 90, 147–48

Oldfield, E. C., Jr. "Barney," 84

Ornstein, Warren, 30

Parke, Jane Neal. *See* Batten, Jane

Parke, Mary Eugenia, 56

Parkinson, Lucius, 26, 29–30

Patterson, Donald H., Jr., 104

Paxon Communications, 141

Peat, Marwick, Mitchell & Co., 93

Pelmorex, 134–35, 162

Perkins, Henry D., 11

Petersburg Progress-Index, 10–11

Portsmouth Star, 10, 54

Portsmouth Times, 54–55

Posey, Ernest L., Jr., 45

Powell, Lewis, 69

Price, Harry, 59

Princeton (W. Va.), 82

Pulitzer Prizes, 63, 75

Purdy, George, 100

racism, 35–37. *See also* school desegregation

Ragged Island Gunning Club, 18

Reagan, Nancy, *photo gallery, 11*

Reagan, Ronald, *photo gallery, 10*

Richmond Time-Dispatch, 10

Rixey, Jack, 76

Roanoke (Va.), 86–87

Roanoke Rapids (N.C.), 81–82

Roanoke Times, 86–87

Robbins, Jim, 86

Roberts, Dick, 82, 85, 130, 171

Rockefeller, John D., III, 41

Roos, John, 23

Rowe, Sandra Mims, 143

Rugaber, Walter, 89

Runte, Roseann, 147

Ryan, Louis, 124, 126

Sackett, Sheldon, 55

Samuel L. Slover Library (Norfolk, Va.), 153

Satellite Transponder Addressable Receiver. *See* Weather STAR

Saunders, Stuart, 69

Saunders, William, 79–80

Schechter, Gary, 110–11
school desegregation, 4, 62–72
Schurz Communications, 88
Sermersheim, Gail, 86
Shadow (yacht), 105–6; *photo gallery, 7*
Shadow Fay (yacht), 100; *photo gallery, 3*
Shadow II (yacht), 101–3
Shadow J (yacht), 100
Shumadine, Conrad, 2, 126
Simpson, Robert, 132
Singer, Mark, 112
Slover, Fay Martin, 10, 14–15, 18, 91, 100, 169
Slover, Henry Clay, 7
Slover, Samuel L., 3, 5, 7–13, 15–16, 22–24, 37, 51, 76, 157; *photo gallery, 2*
Slover Trust, 169
Smith, Betty, 44
Smith, C. Ray, 150
Smith, Dennis, 121
Smith, Rebecca Beach, 127–28
Snider, William M., 43
Stanley, Bahns, 120
Stanley, Thomas, 63
Stanley Plan, 66
Stant, Frederick, Jr. "Bingo," 97–98
Steele, Alexandra, 132
Stevenson, Howard, 4
Stoldal, Bob, 138
Storm Stories, 131
Strong, M. Stuart, 110–11
Sugg, Harold G., 50
Sulzberger, Arthur "Punch," 108

Tarver, Jack, 108
Taylor, Elizabeth, 39–40
Tazewell, E. Bradford, Jr., 17

TeleCable, 3, 82–86, 130, 146, 152
TeleCommunications, Inc., 86, 135
television industry, 96–97, 99, 120, 156, 160; investigative reporting in, 139–40. *See also individual stations (e.g., KLAS-TV, etc.)*
Tesch, Heather, 132
Thatcher, Margaret, *photo gallery, 11*
Thayer, Bill, 24
Thompson, Frank, 45
Thomson, James M., 10
Thornton, Daniel M., 93, 96
Thurmond, Strom, 65
Tidewater Community College, 152, 153
Times-World Corporation, 86–88
Tomlin, Dave, 119
Towers Shopping Center (Roanoke, Va.), 86, 88
Trader Publishing Company, 141, 155–56
Travel Channel, 3, 141
Triad Trading Post, 140
Trump, Donald, 4
Tucker, Henry St. George, 44
Tucker, J. Hobart, 29
Tucker, John H., Jr., 149
Turcol, Tom, 139
Turner, Debbie, 140
Turner, Ted, 5, 84, 104–5, 128

University of Virginia, 149–51, 153

Virginia Industrialization Group, 69
Virginia National Bank, 93, 95–97
Virginian-Pilot, 10, 12, 49, 53, 156, 164; school desegregation and, 4, 62, 64–70, 72, 74–75
Virginia Wesleyan College, 152

Virginia Zoo, 153
Vodrey family, 88
Wahab, Bob, 59–60
Wahrman, Ben, 59
Warren, Robert Penn, 180n6
Washington Post, 81, 116
WDBJ-AM/FM, 86, 88
WDBJ-TV, 86–87
Weather Channel: first year of, 1–3, 120–29; high definition broadcasting and, 131, 156; in international markets, 5, 133–36; sale of, 3, 161–63, 167–68; take off of, 130–36; technology of, 130–31
Weather Channel Interactive, 136, 156, 161
weather.com, 132–33, 136, 161
Weather Services International (WSI), 133–34, 155, 161–62
Weather STAR, 130–31
Webb, Lewis W., Jr., 90
WFMY-TV, 78–79, 88, 137
Willcox, Peter H., 103
Williams, Phil, 139
Wilson, Debora J., 133
Wilson, Harvey Laird, 9–10

Winchester, Lee, 26
Wise, John D., 48
WLBT-TV, 96
WLTY-FM, 137
Wolcott, Eddie, 103
World-News, 86–87
World Series promotions, 17
World's Fair (1939), 100
Worth, Nick, 83
Wright, David McCord, 38
Wright, Jerauld, 60; *photo gallery,* 9
WSI. *See* Weather Services International
WSI In Flight, 133–34
WSI Pilotbrief, 133–34
WTAR-AM/FM, 137
WTAR Radio-TV Corp., 49
WTAR-TV, 96–99, 137
WTVF-TV, 139
Wynne, John O. "Dubby," 4, 123, 127–29, 130

yachting, 100–106

Zanks, Jack, 102
Zucker, Jeff, 163